The New Rules of Retirement Saving

THE RISKS NO ONE IS TELLING YOU ABOUT . . .
AND HOW TO FIX THEM

Martin H. Ruby
with Neil Wilding & Becky Swansburg

Stonewood Financial
LOUISVILLE, KENTUCKY

Martin H. Ruby/Stonewood Financial Solutions
950 Breckenridge Lane, Suite 130
Louisville, KY 40207
www.StonewoodFinancialSolutions.com

Book layout ©2013 BookDesignTemplates.com

Ordering Information:
Quantity sales. For details, contact the address above.

The New Rules of Retirement Saving/ Martin H. Ruby with Neil Wilding & Becky Swansburg. —2nd ed.
ISBN—9781799135289

Contents

Prologue

Y ou're about to read a book written by an actuary.

Wait, don't close the cover.

I know the old stereotypes. What's an actuary? A Certified Public Accountant without the personality. What's a computer? An actuary with a heart.

But the truth is, an actuary is someone who uses math and statistics to assess and minimize risk. And, whether or not you know it, risk is all around you as you save for the future.

So what's an actuary doing writing a book on saving?

In 1998, I was talking to one of my oldest friends as he began getting his assets in order for retirement. At the time, I was chief executive officer of an annuity company, but on the side I was always giving advice to friends and family who needed help figuring out complex financial decisions. As an actuary, I knew how to get deep into financial products and figure out their benefits, so giving my friends some informal advice became a hobby.

On that afternoon in 1998, over a cup of coffee at my office, my friend asked me a question that would change my life: "Do people like *you* ever help people like *me* plan for retirement? I want an actuary to be my advisor."

It was an intriguing question. But I had to answer: "No."

It's a funny thing. Actuaries are uniquely positioned to help you think about saving. Our specialty is discovering risks and figuring out how to eliminate (or at least minimize) them. But the vast majority of actuaries work for large financial or insurance companies in steel and glass towers, where they seldom come into contact with the public. Actuaries spend their time helping institutions, not individuals.

But my friend's question kept ruminating in my head. Could actuaries help individuals?

That simple question was an awakening for me. My "a-ha moment," so to speak. I've always had an entrepreneurial streak to my personality. I love trying things no one has tried before. I realized I could use my actuarial expertise to help individuals instead of corporations. It became my mission and my passion.

In 2001, I founded Stonewood Financial with the goal of bringing actuarial expertise to everyday savers. And while I love helping savers one at a time, this book is my way of helping savers well beyond my clients and friends.

Many people have their own doctor, their own CPA, or even their own attorney. Why not have your very own actuary? Well, now you can.

Help from an Actuary?

An actuary is someone who uses math and statistics to analyze the financial consequences of risk. You'll find our fingerprints on almost all insurance and financial products. Have you ever wondered how your health insurance company determines your premium each year? At some point in the process of designing the policy, an actuary had to calculate the cost of covering your risk of getting sick, getting injured or dying. If the insurance policy protects your property, such as your home or car, an actuary had to crunch the numbers and predict the odds of your home burning to the ground, or your car being involved in an accident.

Wherever you find risk, you'll find actuaries.

Actuaries certainly have a stereotype: we're the geeks of the math world. As one comedian put it: "Actuaries were invented so accountants would have somebody to make fun of."

In a way, we are. Actuaries love numbers. And the thing about numbers is they don't lie. They are absolute. If Johnny has an apple stand and sells five apples a day for three days, he will have sold fifteen apples. Case closed. There is no way to spin that. Life may be complex and fraught with a multitude of problems and uncertainty, but logic is simple and numbers are starkly pure. There is a rare, sweet harmony to math not found in the other sciences.

The English words "actuary" and "actual" stem from the same Latin root, which connotes "a state of fact" or "that which is real." When analyzed correctly, numbers can tell us much about life, especially its financial side. Take Johnny and his apple stand, for instance. As a merchandiser of fruit, he is no superstar. This had better be a sideline for the kid because, at five apples a day, if he has any overhead at all, he is a bankruptcy candidate (of course that may depend on how much he gets per apple). Any financial undertaking held up to the light of analysis by applied actuarial science will have a much better chance of succeeding than one without such benefit.

Your Own Personal Actuary

I believe people should have their own actuary the way they have their own doctor, lawyer or accountant. Actuaries specialize in identifying and reducing risk. And financial risk is what keeps many of us up at night. Will the stock market rise or fall? Will interest rates go up or down? Have I saved money in the right vehicles, with the right tax status, at the right time? It's enough to give anyone insomnia. Just about everyone's financial portfolio could use help mitigating risk.

One of the reasons I founded Stonewood Financial was so I could take the unique science of risk assessment and actuarial problem solving out of the boardroom and bring it into the living room, so to speak. All of us deal with risk in our financial lives — risk that can be mitigated, or at least prepared for, through actuarial analysis.

So let this book be your own personal actuary. I promise it will be more interesting, insightful, and enlightening than our stereotype would lead you to believe.

The New Rules of Retirement Saving

"Invest in the future because that is where you are going to spend the rest of your life." ~ Habeeb Akande

I did it wrong.

That's not easy for a person like me to admit. I'm an actuary. And actuaries are mathematical experts at managing risk.

Yet I was blind to some of the biggest financial risks I'd ever face.

There's a good chance you're doing it wrong, too. This book is an attempt to fix that.

What is the "it" I'm referencing?

Saving for your future.

I know. Not the sexiest topic (except to actuaries like me). But it may be the most important thing you change this year.

So what did I do wrong? I saved for the future in the wrong way.

It wasn't my fault. Not completely, anyway. I had a lot of people — experts among them — encouraging me to save this way. Now, at age sixty-five, I can see the tremendous mistakes I made.

Here's how I got into this predicament.

I graduated from Purdue University in 1972 with a degree in mathematics and physics. I was so eager to start my first job that I skipped my graduation ceremony altogether. While my classmates were tossing their hats in the air, I was settling into a new role as an actuarial student at Traveler's Insurance in Hartford, Connecticut.

At that point, saving for retirement was easy: I didn't have to do it personally because my company did it for me. In the 1970s, Travelers had a defined benefit pension plan, so each year I accrued a portion of my salary that would be paid to me at retirement for the rest of my life. Amazingly, I didn't have to contribute a cent to this plan. It was up to my employer to fully fund it.

If only it had stayed that easy.

By the 1990s, I was CEO of an insurance company called Integrity Life, headquartered in Louisville, Kentucky. And here's where my savings plans went astray.

At Integrity, we didn't have a formal pension program. Instead, we saved in what was, at the time, the hot new savings product in America: the 401(k).

If you're reading this book, chances are you're saving in a 401(k), too. And chances are, if you don't make a change today, you're going to be facing the same risks I am in the future.

It doesn't have to be that way.

Here's the secret most financial experts know, but aren't telling you: today's most popular ways of saving for the future are creating some of the biggest risks in modern financial history. Yes, that includes 401(k)s and Individual Retirement Accounts, or IRAs.

What does that mean? This book will show you.

This book will teach you the **New Rules of Retirement Saving** and how you can use these rules to transform your savings strategy, eliminate risk, and increase your ability to enjoy the relaxing retirement you envision for yourself many years from now.

As you read this book, you may get a sinking feeling as you realize you're saving for retirement in the wrong way. I'm here to tell you, it's not your fault. Our nation's savings infrastructure is slow to react when new risks develop, and most Americans are still saving under the old rules.

But you are responsible for what you do next. So don't save with the strategies of yesterday, strategies that can't overcome the risks of today.

Use these new rules of saving.

When you finish this book, I promise you'll feel more confident, more hopeful, and more prepared about your future and how to save for it.

I promise that if you follow the New Rules of Retirement Saving, you'll never have to start a book by writing, "I did it wrong."

Crisis in America

There's a crisis going on in America today, and you've inadvertently become part of it.

As a country, we have a problem using old financial strategies that no longer work to manage today's financial realities. We are using *old* rules to address *new* problems.

In most areas of life, we've kept up with the times. Certainly no one today takes a photo at the beach with a Kodak camera, drives to the store, drops off the film, waits five days to pick up the prints. Today, you just snap a picture of that sunset on your phone and share it with the world via Instagram. Likewise, if you want to watch a movie on Friday night, you're more likely to order it on demand or via Netflix than to drive to a video store, pick out a DVD (or VHS!) and bring it home.

In fact, we're using new rules for most things we do. Do you bank online? Avoid eating too much red meat? Drive a car with an airbag? Research TVs online before buying one? In all these cases and more, we've recognized that today's reality requires new rules. We've found better, more efficient, more rewarding ways to do many of the things we depend on for a happy life.

But not when we save for retirement. There, the vast majority of us still play by very old rules.

Your retirement savings represent your ability to enjoy a rewarding, happy future. And yet, most of us are using rules that are outdated and, worse, no longer valuable.

Imagine if every time you wanted to take a trip, you had to call the airline and have them mail you a ticket. That's the way it used to work. It's silly to accept that kind of inefficiency today, when you can get tickets electronically in a matter of minutes.

Or imagine if you broke your arm, but didn't use an X-ray to see what's broken. For years, doctors had to guess what kind of fracture you had. Today, no one with access to good medical care would rely on guesses rather than X-rays.

When it comes to saving for retirement, most of us are making do with approaches that are as inefficient as mailing airline tickets and as risky as setting broken bones without X-rays.

It's time to update our rules.

They're All Talking About You

Do you know what they're saying about you? No, not your best friends or work buddies. I'm talking about the media. Fox News. Forbes. The New York Times. USA Today.

It's hard to find a news outlet these days that hasn't weighed in on the "savings crisis" in America. Most workers aren't saving enough for retirement, and you may even be among them. And that means you may be underprepared when your future arrives. Simply put, your retirement could be at risk.

And the media is right . . . to a point.

What the media is missing is that it's not your fault. You and your friends undoubtedly care about your future. You're saving. You're just saving under an *old set of rules*!

And because you're saving under an old set of rules, saving has become so problematic, so unrewarding, that many of your peers have given up all together. The rest of you do it out of obligation, but not with any measurable satisfaction.

This book is a guide to breaking that cycle.

Yes, I'm Talking to YOU

Are you saving in a 401(k) or IRA? Great job! You're doing more than many Americans.

I know it's tempting to say, "This book isn't for me. I already know what I'm doing."

But this book is for you. It's for every saver who has been misled by what's popular in today's savings market, with little regard for whether what's *popular* is also what's *successful.*

My client Andrew is a perfect example.

Andrew is a CPA, and he knows numbers. He also knows how to evaluate risk. After one of our meetings, he remarked to me, "You know, when I first met you, I always assumed you were talking about other people. I figured I was smart enough to know how to save. Heck, I advise my clients on some of the same strategies you're dismissing. But you know what? I needed help, too. I was relying too much on the talking heads and not enough on the level heads."

So before we begin, let me say: I *am* talking to you. I promise. If you're like the vast majority of savers today, no matter how smart you are, you're saving under the old rules.

The Old Rules of Retirement Saving

Save through your employer. Invest in the market. Defer your taxes.

Lots of today's common savings rules were created for a far different kind of saver.

They were created for savers like my Uncle Irwin. Irwin would be eighty-eight this year, and he did something that is pretty foreign to most people reading this book: he worked for the same company *his entire career.* Irwin worked his way up the ranks, from salesman to management and finally to the senior leadership team. As a reward for his decades of loyalty, when Irwin retired, his company gave him a pension. During his later working years, he also saved in a 401(k), which his company matched handsomely.

The current rules of saving were created for people like Irwin. They were created for a time when employers shouldered most of the financial commitment for an employee's retirement fund, either through pensions or high 401(k) matches. My uncle didn't contribute much to his retirement accounts: his pension was entirely funded by his company, and his 401(k) was heavily subsidized by his employer. Most of his annual salary went to daily use, not long-term savings.

If you're reading this book and you have a pension like Irwin, good for you! Keep on saving under the old rules.

If you're reading this book and your employer matches 10 percent or more of your 401(k) contributions like my uncle's did, that's great! Keep saving under the old rules, too.

If you're like most Americans and you're saving for retirement without generous support from your employer, these rules aren't going to work for you.

That's why I've created a new set of rules.

Three Rules for a Better Future

This book is about the New Rules of Retirement Saving. It's about taking the same kind of insights and advancements that have taken place throughout our world, and applying them to retirement saving.

These three rules are based on a blunt assessment of the risks you face today as a saver. Follow them, and you'll be on a better path to saving.

Why three rules? I could have created twenty or thirty new rules, from broad statements on savings philosophy to minutiae about daily savings activities, but I know you're not going to remember twenty rules. Besides, I've found it really boils down to three big actions. And if you take these three actions, you'll be better prepared for retirement . . . not based on the past but based on the present and the future.

So what are the three New Rules of Retirement Saving?

Rule #1: Know Your Risks

Rule #2: Choose a Strategy That Addresses Your Risks

Rule #3: Take Action Now

Sounds simple? It's actually a fundamental shift from the way you're saving today.

Over the rest of this book, I'll help you learn about each rule and put it to work in your own savings strategy. By the end, you'll see how these three simple rules can transform your approach to the future.

Picture You at Seventy-Five

Take a moment to imagine: What will your life be like when you're seventy-five?

No, I'm not talking about the iPhone 84, or getting robots to fold your laundry (which I'm all for, by the way). I'm talking about how you envision yourself living as time goes by. Look through the telescope of the future and allow your mind to focus on what your life will be like then.

This type of future-gazing is something too few of us do, but it's essential to retirement planning.

Here's how I see my life at age seventy-five: My wife and I have sold our current house and moved to something smaller within walking distance of restaurants and shops. When a new restaurant opens, we will be among the first to try it out. I'll continue going to the Broadway theatrical series as a favor to my wife, and she'll continue humoring me by going to University of Louisville men's basketball games with me. Each summer, we'll spend a week on Hilton Head Island with our daughters and grandchildren. We'll travel to visit friends across the country, and maybe even get a condo on the beach in Florida. I'll have more time to volunteer and support organizations that are important to me. And you can bet I'll make as many of my grandkids' soccer games and ballet recitals as I can.

When I think about my life at seventy-five, very little of it has to do with money. And yet, the picture I see can only be supported if I have the income to make it a reality. Will I have the money to go to Hilton Head? Will I be able to give generously to United Way? Will I be able to eat out when I want without worrying too much about what's on the right side of the menu? Or, will I be anxious about fitting an occasional expensive meal into a tight monthly budget?

When people tell me they don't have time to think about their future (let alone save for it), I ask them to go through the same exercise mentioned above. Picture life at seventy-five.

Take a moment and do it yourself. Write down five or six things you want to be sure you'll have. It's okay if these things change over time. The important thing is to picture them now:

At seventy-five, I want to:

What did you write down? Even if you chose not to put anything on those lines, I want you to at least think about it. After all, these are the things that will make up your retirement.

The new rules of saving will make sure the goals on the above list become reality. They can save you from sacrificing pleasures down the road because you didn't plan well today.

"Outside the Box" Thinking

I'm here to give you a new lens through which to view your finances. It's going to feel different than what you've done before.

I'm reminded of a story from the early 1900s when the automobile was just being introduced. A spokesman for Daimler Benz was asked about the future of cars, and he remarked, "There will never be a mass market for motorcars because there is a limit on the number of chauffeurs available." His assumption was, of course, that every car needed a chauffeur. That blinded him to the potential of the personal automobile.

The same is true with savings today. Too many of us are saying, "There's a limit to how successful I can be because there's a limit to the strategies I'm using to save."

As you've probably guessed by now, we're about to blow that assumption out of the water. Let's start with the first New Rule of Retirement Saving: Know Your Risks.

CHAPTER TWO

Rule #1: Know Your Risks

"Risk comes from not knowing what you're doing." ~ *Warren Buffett*

Let's talk risks.

You take risks into account more often than you probably give yourself credit for. Do you wear a seat belt? If you do, you are helping mitigate the risk of a fatal car crash. Do you eat fresh fruits and vegetables? With those wise dietary choices you are helping address the risk of heart disease and other illnesses. Do you check the weather report before you leave the house? That is also a good idea. You're trying to eliminate the risk of getting drenched on your way to lunch.

Those risks are relatively easy to address because it doesn't take much to avoid them (I can buckle up in less than four seconds). Savings risk is different. It takes time to understand, and it takes commitment to change the way you're saving.

Your Three Biggest Risks

A book is sometimes an impersonal medium. When I meet with a client, I get to look at her across the table, get to know his family, or understand their financial situation. So you might be thinking, "How can he know MY biggest risks?"

Here's a secret: almost everyone is struggling with the same three risks. Read the following descriptions and think about whether they apply to you:

No. 1: Structural Risk — This risk is about the mechanics of saving. How are you saving? What savings vehicles are available to you? Who is helping you save? Is your employer contributing to your savings program? If so, how? Are government resources available to you? If so, what are they? Do you know which ones you should take advantage of and how to do so? How is your savings program structured? These questions can make the difference between whether you are successful or not, especially if your goal is to provide a comfortable retirement for yourself.

No. 2: Market Risk — Anyone who has followed the stock market over the last two decades is well aware of this risk. When you are saving money for your future, you want it to grow. Placing money in the stock market for that purpose comes with a risk that can best be illustrated by a pair of scales. Losses on one side. Gains on the other. The market giveth, and the market taketh away. This risk pertains to more than just Wall Street. Any time your savings are invested where loss is possible, whether it be stocks, bonds, real estate, or a host of other assets, you face real risk that your savings will not experience sufficient growth to offset losses.

No. 3: Tax Risk — This risk is quite simple: How much of your retirement account will you get to use, and how much will you give to Uncle Sam in paying taxes? Tax risk is perhaps one of the most underappreciated risks today's savers face, and many Americans are doing nothing to address it. Many seemed resigned to pay any and all taxes presented to them as if there were absolutely nothing they could do about it. They believe Benjamin Franklin, who noted, "In this world nothing can be said to be certain but death and taxes." Or perhaps Will Rogers, who said, "The only difference between death and taxes is that death doesn't get worse every time Congress meets." "The uninformed taxpayer will pay much more in taxes than the informed taxpayer." I said that last one.

More than any other factors, these risks will impact how you save, how your money grows, and, eventually, how you spend your money.

Encountering these risks one at a time is challenging enough, but you have to face all three, right now.

In the next chapters, we'll look at these risks one by one and help you assess how each risk may be impacting your retirement plans.

CHAPTER THREE

Structural Risk

"Money amassed either serves us or rules us." ~ Horace

Let's go back to my Uncle Irwin. In retirement, my uncle loved playing golf. And why not? Irwin had a great life. When he graduated from college, he got a job with a manufacturer, and over the next forty years he slowly climbed the corporate ranks from assistant to manager to division manager to vice president. At age sixty, he retired with a pension that sent him a check for $80,000 every year . . . for the rest of his life. So he didn't have to worry if the stock market was up or down or how much money was left in his retirement account. His company guaranteed him that pension check for life.

No wonder he played so much golf!

You probably know people like Irwin, unless you're under the age of fifty. Then there's a good chance you don't. You see, people like Irwin just don't exist among today's younger generation.

Today's retirement landscape is unlike any in history. And a lot of it has to do with structural risk.

"Structural risk" sounds like an actuarial term, but actually it's a simple concept: This is the risk that comes with the mechanics of saving. What are the vehicles available to you? What are the rules of the saving game? Who is going to help you save?

Let's look at the structural risk that existed for Irwin. He could be your grandparent, parent, or uncle... anyone working and saving in the 1950s, 60s, and 70s.

Here's what Irwin had:

- He had an employer who was saving money for him every month — money that would be paid to him in retirement.
- He had a pension that guaranteed him a hefty portion of his final salary for the rest of his life . . . no matter how long he lived.
- He had the promise of Social Security to supplement his income in retirement.

All in all, I would call that a pretty sweet deal, wouldn't you? Today, these kinds of guarantees are only available to a small portion of workers: firefighters, teachers, and government employees. If you don't fall into one of those categories, I'll show you what you face instead.

The Three-Legged Stool

Irwin's savings approach — and the approach Americans have been relying on for much of the last century — is a three-legged stool. That means the money he relied on in retirement was supported by three "legs" of assets.

Irwin's saving was supported by his employer's contributions, his own savings, and the government through Social Security. Take away any of those three legs, and the stool would wobble and fall over. Irwin didn't have to worry about that, because each of his legs were strong.

Now, think about your own personal savings stool.

Probably, the personal savings leg is doing okay. You know you should be saving and are putting something away each month (right?).

How about the other two legs? Employer and government? Maybe not as strong. Let's look at why.

Leg No. 1: Employer Savings

Pensions are on the endangered species list. There was a time in America that you could land a good job with a big corporation, spend thirty or forty years there, work hard, earn raises and promotions, and then retire with a gold watch and a guaranteed lifetime paycheck. That leg of the stool started to wobble in the 1960s when corporations found it difficult to keep their pension promises.

Defined benefit pension programs were part of the perks and benefits of nearly every employer of any size. It was one way they sought to attract loyal, long-staying employees. As the 1970s moved into the 80s, long-staying employees began to stop mattering so much to corporate America. Fringe benefits became too expensive and administratively burdensome to maintain, so they just began dropping them.

How did things change?

Maybe you've heard about the Studebaker automobile. The Studebaker was ahead of its time. It was the first to come out with innovations like curved windshields, disc brakes, seat belts, and mechanical power steering. For some reason, the fickle American car-buying public just didn't go for them like they did Fords and General Motors cars. So the last Studebaker rolled off the line in 1966.

The United Auto Workers (UAW) had worked hard at the negotiating table. Studebaker workers had excellent pension plans and lush benefits. But when laid-off employees began to collect their pensions, they learned that Studebaker didn't have enough money to pay the benefits.

Howls of protest reached Capitol Hill. Congress was moved to pass the 1974 Employee Retirement Income Security Act (ERISA), which regulated pension plans. The objective of the new legislation was to protect American workers and ensure their pensions were sustainable. However, as so often happens when our government makes laws, the new demands forced corporations to back away from pensions altogether.

Birth of IRAs and 401(k)s

One interesting byproduct of ERISA was a new law that allowed taxpayers to contribute into something called an "Individual Retirement Account," or IRA. Companies liked them, because IRAs took the pressure off the company to plan for an employee's retirement. These new IRAs could grow tax-deferred. The IRS allowed workers to reduce their immediate taxes by funding their retirement accounts *and* they would owe no taxes on the money until they withdrew it! IRAs began popping up like daisies in spring, especially when tax time rolled around.

In 1978, the IRS inadvertently created 401(k) plans when it established a new section of the IRS code that allowed for tax-deferred accumulation. The little paragraph went virtually unnoticed until Ted Benna, a young Pennsylvania benefits consultant, devised a clever way to apply the new law to corporate benefits. Benna realized this piece of the tax code could potentially provide tax benefits for both employees and employers. From one man's discovery, an entire industry was born.

With 401(k)s, employees didn't have to pay any taxes on their savings today. It sounds like the IRS wouldn't like that, but in reality, the IRS saw 401(k)s as an opportunity. After all, these savings accounts were not tax-**free** — they were tax-**deferred**. At some point, after the accounts grew to fruition, the IRS would get its taxes. And it hoped at that time, since the accounts had grown in value, there would be more taxable income than when the money was contributed.

This was a big shift in the dynamics of retirement. The 401(k) put employees in charge of saving for their own retirement. The employer, instead of guaranteeing a pension payout, would now administer a self-funding retirement plan.

This is the great shift from defined *benefit* to defined *contribution.* Think about that change in wording for a moment. It is not merely a matter of semantics. What is the difference?

Defined benefit: the old pension plans have a defined benefit you would receive every month. The outcome is guaranteed. You get a check for $80,000, for example, every year for the rest of your life.

Defined contribution: 401(k)s and 403(b)s have a defined participation amount. There's a guarantee on the amount of money that will go into the account each month, but there are no guarantees on how much it will grow or — more importantly — how much money you will have at your retirement.

We went from being assured income in retirement to only being assured of a *structure* in which we could save.

The problem with defined contribution plans is that many of the contributions aren't so well defined.

Originally, employer contributions to 401(k) plans were pretty high. That's why they were considered "defined contribution" plans: the employer was putting in a defined amount. In the beginning, most employers contributed a "match" to their employee's 401(k) accounts. That is, if you put in $10, your company might put in $10 and help you save for retirement. This kept 401(k)s more closely aligned with pension plans. Sure, you didn't get a guarantee under a 401(k), but the employer was still contributing a large portion of a worker's retirement funds.

That's often not the case today.

Employer contributions have fallen across the country, with many employers contributing less or not at all.

Today, few employers are matching at meaningful rates.[1] In fact, 82 percent of Americans have either no 401(k), a 401(k) with no match or a 401(k) with a match less than three percent.[2]

Put another way, only 18 percent of Americans have the old standard of meaningful participation by their employer.

This is why the employer leg of your retirement savings stool is probably less stable for you than it was for the generations before you.

How You Save Today

The two most common ways to save for retirement today are 401(k)s and IRAs, and their Roth counterparts. This is what most American workers rely on to build the employer leg of their stool. As we're about to see, both have some significant shortcomings when it comes to creating a strong base for your retirement.

Let's look at the non-Roth version first.

Your account may be called an SEP (simplified employee pension), an IRA or a 401(k). Whatever it's called, it's likely structured the same way. Here are the basics:

- 401(k)s are tax-deferred savings vehicles. Tax-deferred means you deduct your contributions from your taxable income in the

---

[1] Brian O'Connell. The Street. May 02, 2013. "More U.S. Firms Shutter 401(k)s, Matching Programs." http://www.thestreet.com/story/11911313/1/more-us-firms-shutter-401ks-matching-programs.html.

[2] Emily Brandon. U.S. News and World Report. July 1, 2013. "How to Tell if You Have a Lousy 401(k) Plan." http://money.usnews.com/money/retirement/articles/2013/07/01/how-to-tell-if-you-have-a-lousy-401k-plan.

year you make your contributions. If you make $100 a year and contribute $10 to a 401(k), the IRS bases your taxes on $90 of income rather than the full $100.

- Your contributions and all the earnings in your 401(k) are then taxed when you withdraw the funds in retirement. So if you take $100 out of your 401(k) in retirement, you may only get a check for $60 once taxes are paid. Remember: you pay not only federal taxes, but state and local taxes as well.

- Most 401(k) assets are invested in mutual funds and other funds tied to the stock market. This means 401(k)s tend to do well when the market does well and suffer when the market collapses. Other savers invest their 401(k)s in bonds, or some mixture of the two. Bonds can come with their own sets of risks when interest rates are low like today.

- There are also many regulations around 401(k)s. If you access any of the money in your account before age fifty-nine-and-one-half, you'll have to pay a 10 percent penalty on top of the taxes you owe.

- And the government requires you to start withdrawing money at age seventy-and-one-half. Why, you may ask? Because it wants to begin taxing those assets.

- There are limits to how much money you can contribute each year. In 2019, that amount is $19,000 a year for savers under the age of fifty.[3]

- And finally, like all financial products, there are fees built in to 401(k)s, both from the plan administrator and from the individual mutual funds within the account. These fees run around 1 or 2 percent, which may not seem like a lot until you do the math. If your account earns 6 percent this year, you could only net 4 percent after fees. Let's say you're sixty and have amassed

---

[3] IRS. November 1, 2018. "401(k) Contribution Limit Increases to $19,000 for 2019; IRA Limit Increases to $6,000." https://www.irs.gov/newsroom/401k-contribution-limit-increases-to-19000-for-2019-ira-limit-increases-to-6000.

$1 million in your account. Those two percent fees now cost you $20,000 a year.

IRAs and 401(k)s are the most common retirement savings vehicles today, but their Roth counterparts are gaining on them.

Every so often, Congress gets something right, and that was the case when they created the Roth 401(k) and Roth IRA. These accounts work a little differently when it comes to taxation:

- Funds are contributed with post-tax dollars, meaning this account is not tax-deferred. So if you make $100, and contribute $10 to a Roth, the IRS still taxes you on all $100 of income.
- Because savers have already paid taxes on their contributions, their funds grow tax-free. That means you do not owe any more taxes on the funds in your account. This includes all the earnings you've accumulated as your account has grown over the years. If you take $100 out of your account during retirement, you'll get a check for all $100.
- Taxation is the main difference between a Roth and a traditional account. However, many other features are the same as traditional 401(k)s. There is still a 10 percent tax penalty on any earnings withdrawn before age fifty-nine-and-one-half, though contributions can be taken out at any time.
- These accounts are still often linked to the market through mutual funds, meaning when the

Does your three-legged stool look like this?

market crashes, so can account values.

- There are still limits on how much money you can contribute each year, and even limits on who can have a Roth.
- The fees are similar to their traditional counterparts: 1 to 2 percent a year.

If you're thinking, "Gee, neither of these options sounds all that great," you're not alone. Many savers are frustrated with the options available to them.

That's because in both Roths and traditional accounts, the burden of savings has shifted from the employer and a pension to you and however you decide to save. Regardless of the account type you choose, the responsibility is on you, not your company.

So we know the employer leg of your stool is weak. Now you have you and the government left holding up your stool. How strong is the government's leg?

Social (In)Security

Social Security is the way our government participates in your retirement income. Each paycheck you receive has a portion withheld for Social Security, in return for the benefit you're promised in the future.

Should you count on Social Security to help fund your retirement?

Maybe not. I'll explain why.

Below is a paragraph the Social Security Administration is inserting into the text on page one of every Social Security statement they send:

> *"Social Security is a compact between generations. Since 1935, America has kept the promise of security for its workers and their families. Now, however, the Social Security system is facing serious financial problems, and*

action is needed soon to make sure the system will be sound when today's younger workers are ready for retirement. Without changes, in 2033 the Social Security Trust Fund will be able to pay only about 77 cents for each dollar of scheduled benefits."

Seventy-seven cents on the dollar? That's a pretty dire outlook.

So why the warnings? Demographics, demographics, demographics.

Here's the thing: when most people think of Social Security, they think of some pot of money in Washington that the government gives out to retirees each month.

If you were to actually fly to Washington and look in the Social Security Trust Fund, you'd mostly find a bunch of IOUs. Social Security is paid from the current Social Security taxes collected. This is why demographics matter.

In 1960, there were five tax-paying workers supporting each Social Security beneficiary. That means five people were paying the taxes to deliver one Social Security check to one senior citizen. Not too bad.

By 2009, that demographic had shifted dramatically. That year, there were three-and-one-half workers supporting each Social Security beneficiary.

Imagine a pyramid with five people holding up a single person. Not too hard. Now try to hold up that same person with only three helpers, and it gets a little harder.

By 2020, it's expected there will be only two workers for every Social Security beneficiary, meaning you and your spouse are basically paying taxes to support one retiree all by yourselves.

Your pyramid is looking pretty weak, right?

That's why many experts have questioned whether today's Social Security system is sustainable for the future.

What's causing these dramatic demographic shifts? Our U.S. population is aging . . . fast. Seniors are living longer than ever before, and couples are having fewer babies as well. That means we're creating more retirees, but fewer future workers to pay Social Security taxes.

An average of 10,000 baby boomers retired every day. In retirement, they'll start receiving their Social Security checks.[4]

A report by the Social Security Administration summed it up like this: "[After] 2015, almost 33 percent of our workforce, including 48 percent of our supervisors, will be eligible to retire."[5]

Nearly a third of our workforce is eligible to retire!

Younger generations are going to have to work VERY hard to support them all.

When I ask clients who are in their forties and fifties about Social Security, most answer, "It will be great if I get it, but I'm sure not counting on it."

It's a good stance to take if you're under sixty. Because when you have two workers supporting one retiree, you can't deliver the same benefits as when nine workers were supporting that same retiree.

Balancing Your Stool

With the employer leg and government leg of your stool sawed off (or at least sawed much shorter!), people like you are trying to balance on the one remaining leg: what you alone are able to save.

---

[4] Glenn Kessler. The Washington Post. July 24, 2014. "Fact Checker: Do 10,000 baby boomers retire every day?" http://www.washingtonpost.com/blogs/fact-checker/wp/2014/07/24/do-10000-baby-boomers-retire-every-day.

[5] Social Security Administration. 2012. "Annual Performance Plan for Fiscal Year 2013." http://www.ssa.gov/performance/2013/FY%202013%20APP%20and%20Revised%20Final%20Performance%20Plan%20for%20FY%202012.pdf.

Your three-legged stool is now, in essence, a one-legged stool. I like to call it a barstool (and not just because this discussion may lead you to drink!).

Help! I Need Somebody!

A final structural risk many Americans face is financial advice and assistance.

I'm always amazed by this conversation, which I have with almost every new client who comes into our office.

Me: So how is your 401(k) currently invested?

Client: Um, I'm not really sure.

Me: Is it in mutual funds?

Client: Yes, mutual funds.

Me: Which ones?

Client: Um, I'm not sure.

Me: Large cap, growth stocks, bonds, emerging markets? Target-date funds?

Client: I'm not really sure. Whatever they told me I should be in.

Me: Well, how's your account doing? How's it done these past few years?

Client: I'm not really sure. I try not to look at it.

Did that hit a little too close to home? If it did, don't be ashamed. The majority of savers respond in a similar way.

Here's the big problem with today's savings culture. You are really on your own. Today's savers have been put in charge of growing their own retirement funds. In the past, someone managed a company's pension fund. Those people — financial experts — were in charge of making sure there were enough assets to cover a retiree's pension check.

Today, *you* have to be that expert. And most of us don't have the financial background, training or time to make those decisions; 401(k)s — and investing in general — can be very complicated. It doesn't help that your employer probably doesn't offer any advice because they're concerned with the legal ramifications of a human resources department offering employees financial advice.

In short, American businesses have bought in to a savings structure that has transferred much of the risk in saving for retirement from institutions to you as the individual. It's no wonder so many savers are looking for something better.

Advice From Time Magazine

So what should you take away from all this? *Time* magazine put it best in an article by Dan Kadlec: "It's time to recognize that your retirement security is in your hands alone." Today's generations must depend on themselves to save for the future.

In the article, entitled, "Why Your 401(k) Match Will Get Cut," Kadlec made the following observation about the future of retirement in America:

> *"We have a retirement savings crisis in America and the safety net keeps being eaten away. Social Security is a mess. Public and private pension plans are underfunded. We've moved squarely away from secure defined-benefits plans towards riskier defined-contribution plans, and now defined-contribution plans are under assault."*[6]

---

[6] Dan Kadlec. Time. Dec. 13, 2012. "Why Your 401(k) Match Will Get Cut." http://business.time.com/2012/12/13/why-your-401k-match-will-get-cut/.

So what is the takeaway from all of this? Don't expect your employer to take care of you. Don't expect the government to take care of you. You have to do it on your own. That's at the heart of structural risk.

CHAPTER FOUR

Market Risk

"The difference between playing the stock market and playing the horses is that one of the horses must win." ~ Joey Adams

There are a lot of things I don't miss from the 1990s. Flip phones that could barely text. Beanie Babies that somehow convinced millions of adults to buy stuffed animals. Windows 95.

But one thing from the 90s I miss every day is the stock market.

The 1990s were real go-go years in the market. You could pick almost any stock and it would go up. You could actually invest in something called "Dart Funds," where a stockbroker threw a dart at a sheet of stocks and invested in whichever ones the dart hit. And you know what? Dart Funds were making good money!

We all know where the go-go years of the 1990s ended: the dot-com bubble burst. And boy, did that bubble burst hard in 2000. According to Investopedia, from March 11, 2000, to October 9, 2002, the technology-heavy NASDAQ lost 78 percent of its value, falling from 5046.86 at its peak and bottoming at 1114.11, when the implosion ended. The troubles of the stock market were not limited to just technologies. The S&P 500®, the barometer by which the health of the overall stock market is often measured, fell by nearly 40 percent.[7]

My friends who were thinking of retiring around the year 2000 truly understand the concept of "market risk." In January they thought they had $1 million to retire on, and by December their accounts were depleted. A few bad years in the market had wiped out what it had taken them years to save. The hit was so bad, a common joke was that 401(k)s had become 201(k)s.

But there's more to market risk than how much is in your account when you go to retire. A bad market crash can hurt, but so can years of underperformance in the market.

The truth is, almost all of our retirement security is in some way tied to market performance. 401(k)s and IRAs are extremely susceptible to market swings, particularly for younger savers, who are encouraged to put more of their money into funds exposed to the stock market. That introduces a huge level of uncertainty into our best-laid savings plans.

The Worst Decade in Market History

Imagine you had to save during the worst decade in modern U.S. market history. A market so bad, you would, on average, lose money every year. A market that saw not just one, but two crashes that wiped out more than a third of your savings' value.

We feel for our parents and grandparents who had to live through the Great Depression. But here's a surprise: their generation isn't the only one that grew up during one of the worst markets in history. Yours did, too.

Years 2000 through 2009 are estimated to be the single worst decade for the S&P 500®. You might have heard it called the "lost

---

[7] Andrew Beattie. Investopedia. "Market Crashes: The Dotcom Crash." http://www.investopedia.com/features/crashes/crashes8.asp.

decade of investing," because the market ended the decade pretty much at the same point it started.

How bad was it? For those number geeks like me, this next section will be very exciting. If you're not a numbers person, I promise I'll put it in words you can understand, too.

The S&P 500® Total Return: 2000-2018

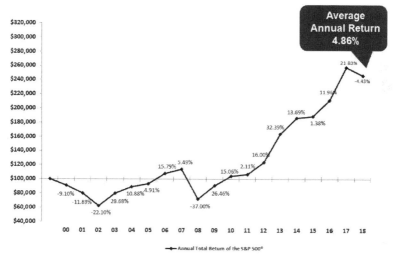

Source: Yahoo Finance GSPC Historical Prices 2019

Let's look at the S&P 500®, a measurement of the 500 largest stocks in the market and an index many people reference when talking about what the "market" did today.

If you had a 401(k) with $100,000 in it, completely invested in the S&P 500®, what would have happened over the first decade of this century? Well, look at the line on the chart above marked, "Annual Total Return of the S&P 500." This represents your account value. The market crashes from 2000 to 2002. It takes you four years to earn back what you've lost, and finally by 2006 you're above water. Then, in 2008 you lose it all again.

You saw some good years. The market was up 28 percent in 2003, and 26 percent in 2009. But you used those big gains to earn back the money you had lost when the market dropped. So those gains really didn't reflect forward progress, did they?

In fact, it's even less progress than you think.

What do you think your 401(k) earned, on average, from 2000 through 2009, if it was invested in "the market"? Four percent? Three percent?

The answer is worse than you think. It's *negative* 1 percent. That's right. For the entire decade, you lost about 1 percent per year.

That is a frightening way to grow your retirement savings.

The experience over the rest of the century hasn't been much better. From 2000 through the end of 2014, the S&P 500® has returned an average of a little more than 4 percent per year. Not terrible (at least you didn't *lose* money), but also not enough to grow your account value in a meaningful way. And remember, that 4 percent is your growth before you pay the fees inside your 401(k) or IRA, and of course before Uncle Sam takes out a chunk for taxes.

No one is going to successfully retire on an account that's growing in the low single digits. You need meaningful growth to fuel your account.

Why It Hurts So Much When the Market Crashes

Here's a very concrete example of why most savers weren't celebrating when the market rose 28 percent in 2003. Below is a chart of the growth needed for recovery when the market drops:

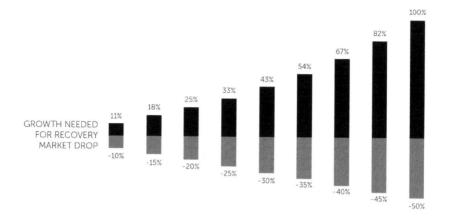

That's right. If the market drops 50 percent, your account needs to grow by 100 percent to make up that loss. So when the market dropped 22 percent in 2002, and went up 28 percent in 2003, many savers were still under water: they hadn't earned back everything they had lost.

Let's put it another way. You have $10. You lose 50 percent of it. Now you have $5. You grow that money by 50 percent. Now you have $7.50. You're still $2.50 short of where you started.

Chasing Growth

There's one simple question I like to ask new clients about their retirement savings: How much do you expect to earn on your retirement savings this year?

Guess which one is the most common response I hear from clients:

a) 9 percent
b) 7 percent
c) 4 percent
d) I have no idea

If you guessed D, you're right. C is a close second. Or rather a variation on C: "I don't know, maybe 3 or 4 percent? Right now, I'm just happy if I'm not losing money."

Now you know why.

Here's the thing. If your 401(k) or IRA is invested in mutual funds (and most of them are), this is going to be your experience. Most mutual funds do not beat the S&P 500®, and the numbers above don't take into account expenses, either.

I've seen this problem firsthand.

My oldest daughter graduated from college in 2001 and started saving just as the market was crashing. Her account has followed the performance of the market very closely. She has earned an average of about 3.8 percent per year in the time she had been saving. Her 401(k) plan charges around a 1 percent management fee. Subtract another 1 percent for the mutual funds in which she is invested. Net to her, she has earned about 1.8 percent this century on her savings.

That's simply not enough to fund her retirement goals. It's causing her a lot of sleepless nights.

Like you, my daughter is depending on the market to grow her nest egg. She's coming to realize, unless something changes, the market may not be able to give her enough forward growth to fund the retirement she wants.

Let's face it: the market of today isn't the market of the 1990s. No one is throwing darts and hoping for great stock returns.

Low Interest Rates and You

So if the stock market is too risky a way to grow your money, how else can you grow it?

Traditionally, people have used "safer" alternatives, like CDs, money market funds, and even basic savings accounts to grow money they want to keep safe. My son-in-law is a great example of this. He has no tolerance for losing money, so a big portion of his 401(k) is invested in government bonds, a very secure asset that's unlikely to lose money. Despite having $50,000 in his 401(k), last year he earned just $1,200. Why? Because low interest rates have dampened the return he can get off safe vehicles like government bonds.

I'm going to tell you a story that sounds unbelievable, but I promise you, it's true.

When I was in my thirties, I opened a checking account at a local bank in Louisville, Kentucky. It was a basic account, a place to deposit my salary and write checks to cover our bills. (This was the 1980s. You actually had to write a check, put it in an envelope and mail it to pay your bill.)

I was very careful about when I paid my bills. I always waited until the last possible day.

This odd behavior wasn't because I was broke: I had plenty of money to cover what I owed. But I was still very concerned about timing. You see, in 1980, my checking account had an interest rate of around 18 percent.

Yes, you read that right: 18 percent.

That meant the money in my account was earning at an annuitized rate of 18 percent interest every day. Naturally, I wanted to keep money in the account as long as possible. And that meant paying my bills on the very last day they were due.

What's your checking account earning today?

There's a good chance you don't know. And really, there's no reason to know. Because the interest you're earning on your money is pretty inconsequential.

Most checking accounts today earn somewhere around 0.05 percent to 0.10 percent. Take note of where the decimal point is. It's not a good time to grow your savings off interest.[8]

---

[8] Bankrate. "Checking & Savings." http://www.bankrate.com/checking.aspx.

Low interest rates have been a boon for borrowers. Auto loans? Less than 2 percent. Mortgage loans? Less than 6 percent.

But the same low interest rates that make it easy to buy a car or finance a home have made it very challenging to grow wealth safely.

The New Norm?

Most safe alternatives to the stock market rely on interest rates. And low interest rates are here to stay . . . at least in the near term.

Interest rates have been falling steadily since the mid-1980s and are currently at historic lows. There are some clear reasons why this trend is likely to continue.

In a 2014 speech to the International Monetary Fund, then-Federal Reserve Chairman Janet Yellen commented, "I do not presently see a need for monetary policy to deviate from a primary focus on attaining price stability and maximum employment."[9]

Granted, that's a lot of Washington-speak. Translated to the English you and I speak every day, our government is saying interests rates should stay low because we want companies to be able to afford to hire workers and we want workers to be able to afford to buy bread, milk, cars, and clothes at prices that aren't pumped up by inflation. And we've seen that to be true.

[9] Janet L. Yellen. Chair of the Board of Governors of the Federal Reserve System. July 2, 2014. "Monetary Policy and Financial Stability." Speech given at the 2014 Michel Camdessus Central Banking Lecture, International Monetary Fund, Washington, D.C. http://www.federalreserve.gov/newsevents/speech/yellen20140702a.htm.

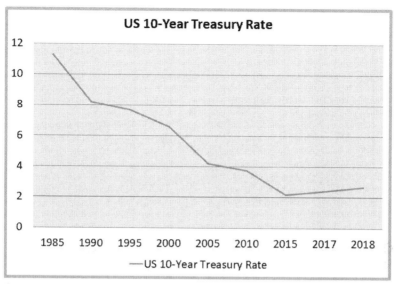

US 10-Year Treasury Rate

Source: U.S. Treasury – Treasury Yield Rates

There's another reason rates could stay low.

The government wants — and needs — low interest rates.

The U.S. government has a big incentive to help keep interest rates low: it reduces Uncle Sam's debt payments. An increasingly large portion of our federal budget each year goes to paying interest on the U.S. debt. In 2010, 6 percent of our federal budget was dedicated to debt service, or around $209 billion. By 2035, the Congressional Budget Office projects debt service will grow to 25 percent of the budget, or around $2.27 trillion. As this book is written, the federal government is borrowing and repaying money at very low interest rates. If those rates rise, so does our national debt. Consider this: between 2011 and 2013, the gross federal debt rose more than $3 trillion. If interest rates had been just 1 percent higher during that time, the government would owe an additional $30 billion in interest each year.

As of June 1, 2005, the total national debt was $7,775,753,817,632.01. Ten years later, June 1, 2015, it was $18,152,841,401,259.20 — more than double.[10] Politicians like to talk about slowing the growth of our national debt, but few hope to reverse the trend altogether.

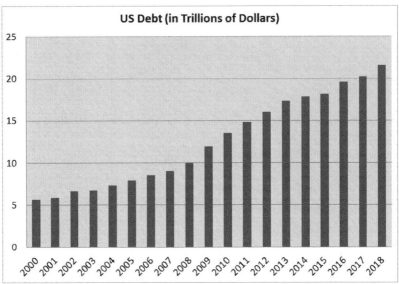

Source: U.S. Department of Treasury, National Debt

Why Low Interest Rates Matter

Alright, I get it. You're not trying to save for retirement through your checking account. (I mean, you're not, right?) But here's why low interest rates matter to you.

In the last section, we looked at the historic volatility the stock market has seen this century. For people not willing to take big risks with their retirement savings, the market isn't a great choice.

---

[10] Treasury Direct. "The Debt to the Penny and Who Holds It." http://www.treasurydirect.gov/NP/debt/current.

So what's the alternative? Safer instruments, like bonds. But in today's low-interest rate environment, safer instruments can't earn enough growth to make them reasonable market alternatives. Remember my son-in-law and the $1,200 he earned on government bonds?

Many savers are asking themselves: What's worse? Making and losing money over and over again in the market, or not making much money at all each year in safer options?

Neither one is likely to be a successful approach.

Your Market Risk

As I said, market risk is all about how you get the money you're saving to grow. The double-punch of a volatile stock market and low interest rates have made that harder for you today than in years past.

There's one more risk that may hit you even harder than a roller-coaster market. That is tax risk.

CHAPTER FIVE

Tax Risk

"The taxpayer: That's someone who works for the federal government, but doesn't have to take a civil service examination." ~ Ronald Reagan

You're doing the right thing: working hard, saving for the future. Who will get to spend the money you've been saving? You will. Perhaps your spouse or children. And certainly the government.

The government, you ask? Ah, taxes.

Tax risk is one of the most important — and least recognized — risks you face. The truth is, after market performance, taxes are probably the biggest variable in your savings plans. Yet, it's a part of retirement planning that young savers are almost never told about.

Get ready to pull back the curtain. By the end of this chapter, you'll never look at taxes the same way again.

The Million Dollar Question

Do you think taxes are going up or down in the future?

I've asked that question a thousand times in the past year, and nearly every single person has answered the same way: Up.

Why do people — young, old, and in between — feel so strongly that taxes are going up? And what does it mean for your retirement account?

How Are You Going to Pay Off All That Debt, Sam?

Uncle Sam's in trouble.

The federal debt is rising and rising. In the last chapter, we talked about how this was a good incentive for the government to keep interest rates low. It's also a good incentive for the government to raise taxes.

How bad is it?

In 2013, analysts were excited that the federal deficit that year would be the first deficit in five years to increase by less than $1 trillion.[11]

It was considered great news that our deficit was *only* going to grow by $1 trillion. One TRILLION dollars. A one with 12 zeroes: $1,000,000,000,000.

Twenty years ago, no one even spoke in terms of trillions. That wasn't even a unit of measurement most people knew. Billions used to be a mind-blowing amount of debt. And now we measure in trillions!

Here's how big a trillion really is, perfectly summed up on the blog "Thoughts You Should Know":[12]

> *"A trillion dollars is so large a number that only politicians can use the term in conversation... probably because they seldom think about what they are really saying. I've read that mathematicians do not even use the term trillion!*

---

[11] Congressional Budget Office. Feb. 5, 2013. "The Budget and Economic Outlook: Fiscal Years 2013 to 2023." http://www.cbo.gov/publication/43907.

[12] Thought You Should Know News. "What's the difference between a million, a billion, a trillion?" http://www.tysknews.com/Depts/Taxes/million.htm.

"Here is some perspective on TRILLION: the country has not existed for a trillion seconds. Western civilization has not been around a trillion seconds. One trillion seconds ago — 31,688 years — Neanderthals stalked the plains of Europe."

Starting around the year 2020—as soon as next year—some analysts expect the U.S. public debt to rise sharply. Because, as we mentioned in chapter three, more and more baby boomers will be retiring and drawing on Social Security and Medicare. The government will owe more people benefits, but not have more revenue (i.e., taxes) coming in. That's going to cause a big imbalance.[13]

Someone is going to have to pay for this mess. That someone is you.

Before we go on, let me make one thing clear: I'm an actuary, not a CPA. I'm not offering you professional tax advice, I'm just educating you on some risks and realities around taxes and your retirement funds. Be sure to consult with your CPA or accountant if you have specific questions pertaining to your savings plans.

Magic Ball: How Taxes Could Hurt Your Savings

If you don't believe me that taxes are going up, consider one of my clients, Mattie. Mattie owns a catering company. She's very successful, catering not only weddings and special events but a growing number of corporate lunches and dinners in our community.

A few years ago at tax time, Mattie discovered she owed $1,266 more in taxes than she planned. She didn't have more income than the year before: profits from her catering company were strong, but flat. And she knew her tax bracket hadn't changed. There had been

---

[13] Jackie Calmes. New York Times. Sept. 17, 2013. "Budget Office Warns That Deficits Will Rise Again Because Cuts Are Misdirected." http://www.ny-times.com/2013/09/18/us/congressional-budget-office-predicts-unsustainable-debt.html?_r=0.

no new tax increases announced by Congress. So she was more than a little confused.

Her accountant cleared it up for her: In the Affordable Care Act (otherwise known as Obamacare), there was a provision to increase the threshold for Social Security taxes. Mattie now owed Social Security taxes on a large part of her income, and, accordingly, her tax bill was higher.

Since 2012, the federal government has raised taxes on capital gains and dividends, Medicare surtax, payroll taxes and taxes for higher earners. That's in the last few years alone.

Taxes penalize successful people like you. If you work hard and make more money, you pay more taxes. You pay local, state and federal taxes, but by far the biggest chunk of that is federal tax, so that's what we'll focus on in this chapter.

First, let's talk about ways your taxes could go up. Then, we'll talk about how this could hurt your retirement accounts.

There are four ways your taxes could go up.

No. 1: The government raises tax rates:

Here's the most common way people think taxes rise. Today, a couple making $200,000 pays a 24 percent marginal tax rate on their income. But Congress could change the rules, and in the future that same couple making that same $200,000 could pay a 30 percent tax rate on their income.

In fact, we know taxes are going up in the future, because they are artificially low today. In December 2017, Congress passed the most sweeping overhaul of the U.S Tax Code we've seen in nearly 30 years. It reduced the marginal tax rate for many savers, and because of it, many of us today are in lower tax brackets than we were a few years ago.

But those tax brackets don't last forever! They are a temporary adjustment. As Congress often does, it included sunset provisions in the bill. That means, in the future, the tax cuts expire and revert back to the old levels. In fact, most household tax provisions in the new law sunset in 2025. So, you can plan on tax rates rising in the near future unless Congress acts again to keep them low.

Married, Filing Jointly[14]		
Income	Previous Tax Rate	New Tax Rate
$160,000	28%	22%
$250,000	33%	24%
$500,000	39.6%	35%

No. 2: You make more money: This is a good problem to have. Today, you're making $60,000 and paying at the 22 percent tax rate. Then you get a promotion and a raise. Now you're making $85,000 and paying at the 24 percent tax rate. You're making more money, which is great. But you owe more of it to the government as well.

It's worth remembering that tax rates are not adjusted for inflation. Many companies give their employees cost-of-living adjustments. They look at the consumer price index — an average of how much it costs to buy things like groceries, clothes and cars — and try to keep their employees' purchasing power level through salary increases. Tax rates don't do that. Your $85,000 will be taxed the same no matter how much (or how little) it can buy for you relative to the past.

No. 3: Your deductions are eliminated: Workers like you have lots of tax deductions you can take. Do you have kids? There's a child tax credit for that. Do you pay interest on your mortgage? You can potentially deduct that, too. But there's a trend in Washington toward taking away those deductions. Put another way, you

---

[14] U.S. Internal Revenue Service via the Motley Fool. Dec. 29, 2017. "Your Complete Guide to the 2018 Tax Changes." https://www.fool.com/taxes/2017/12/29/your-complete-guide-to-the-2018-tax-changes.aspx.

could have to pay taxes on a larger part of your income. Call it what you wish, but that's a tax increase.

Let's say you make $80,000, but with deductions and credits your total taxable income becomes $72,000. If those deductions go away, you'll essentially have $8,000 more dollars on which you must now pay taxes. That means you could owe $2,000 extra dollars in taxes.

No. 4: They tax more things: This is another way the government could tax more of your income. Here's a good example. You don't pay Social Security taxes on every dollar you make. There's a limit, called the Maximum Taxable Earnings. In 2014, the Social Security taxable earnings cap was $117,000. That meant if you made $90,000, you paid Social Security taxes on all of it, but if you made $120,000, you paid taxes only on the first $117,000. In that case, $3,000 would not be subject to Social Security tax.

Things changed in 2015, however. The maximum taxable earnings for Social Security increased to $118,500. So if you earned $120,000 in 2015, you no longer avoided taxes on $3,000, only on $1,500. You pay more in taxes despite your income staying the same.[15]

Deciding When to Pay: Taxes and Your Retirement Accounts

As you can see, there's a lot you can't control about taxes. One thing you CAN control is when you pay — when it comes to retirement savings, at least.

No matter which approach you choose, all the money you save will be taxed in some way. But *how* it is taxed and *when* it is taxed depends on the vehicle you're using to save it. There are two primary ways you can save for retirement. Let's look at them both.

Below is a 101 guide to how taxes are handled in retirement assets. If you already know the difference between a 401(k) and a Roth

---

[15] Social Security Administration. 2015. "Benefits Planner: Maximum Taxable Earnings (1937 – 2015)." http://www.ssa.gov/planners/maxtax.html.

401(k), feel free to skip to the next section. Or, read on for a brush-up.

In long-term savings, there are two ways you can handle taxes, which I've outlined below.

Defer Your Taxes

To defer means to postpone. With this approach, you save for retirement tax-deferred, meaning you do not pay any taxes *today* on the money you set aside for retirement. As that money grows, you pay no annual taxes on the growth. When you finally use the money in retirement, you pay taxes on all the money you withdraw from the account according to your tax rate at that time.

- **Vehicles**: Many of your traditional retirement vehicles use a tax-deferred approach. 401(k)s, IRAs, 403(b)s and most government savings plans (like TSPs) are tax-deferred retirement savings plans.
- **Pluses**: You can deduct contributions in the year you make them, lowering your overall taxable income that year. For some people, their tax rate could be lower in retirement than it is today, making it wise to defer paying those taxes.
- **Minuses**: All the money you grow from the day you start saving until retirement will be taxed. If your $20,000 deposit grows to $100,000, you will owe taxes on the entire $100,000 when you withdraw it.

Pay Your Taxes Upfront

With this approach, you pay taxes upfront before you put the money into a savings vehicle. As the money grows and is spent in the future, you do not owe any additional taxes: not on the money you've contributed, nor on the growth. Sometimes this approach is called "tax-free accumulation," because the money accumulating in your account is never taxed.

- **Vehicles**: Several types of vehicles allow for this approach. Roth 401(k)s and Roth IRAs are two of the most common, along with the savings in certain life insurance vehicles.
- **Pluses**: All accumulation within the policy is tax-free. If your $20,000 contribution grows to $100,000, you'll never pay taxes on the $80,000 gain. Many professionals do not expect to be in a lower tax bracket when they retire, so it makes sense for them to pay taxes upfront.
- **Minuses**: You cannot deduct contributions today to lower your taxable income during your contribution years.

It can be hard to make a decision about which way you want to save from reading the brief descriptions above. After all, these descriptions don't take into account the variables that can happen with regard to taxes . . . your tax risk.

What Happens If . . .

Deciding whether to save tax-free or tax-deferred comes down to one question that may seem pretty hard to answer: Will you pay less OVERALL taxes by paying your taxes today or in the future?

While no one can predict the future, I'm about to show you why there's a good chance you can answer the question above.

First, let's consider what happens to your savings if taxes go up or down.

Tax-Deferred

If you're saving money in a 401(k) or traditional IRA, you will pay taxes when you withdraw the funds in retirement. For example, if you are sixty-five years old and withdrawing $100,000 annually from your retirement account, and you are paying around 30 percent in state and federal income tax, you'll get to keep $70,000 and the government takes $30,000.

If your taxes are higher in the future than they are today, you could end up paying more in taxes than you saved when you deposited the funds.

If your taxes are lower when you withdraw the funds in retirement, then you will be paying less in taxes when you access your money than you would have paid when you deposited the money. That is one reason the tax-deferred approach is often recommended for individuals who believe their tax burden will be significantly lower in the future than it is today.

Either way — whether your tax rate is higher or lower — you will still need to pay taxes on all the growth within your account in a tax-deferred savings program.

If you have a 401(k), every single penny in it will be taxed when you withdraw the money.

Upfront Taxes

If you're saving money using an approach that pays taxes upfront, like a Roth 401(k) or Roth IRA, taxes could impact you differently. If your tax rate is higher when you withdraw your funds in retirement, you will avoid paying that higher tax rate, as you can access your funds tax-free.

If your tax rate is lower when you access your funds in retirement, there is a potential discrepancy between the tax rate you paid upfront on your deposits and the tax rate you could have paid instead when accessing the funds. This is one reason this approach is often recommended for individuals who believe their tax burden will be higher in the future than it is today.

Keep in mind that either way — whether your tax rate is higher or lower — all of the accumulated growth in your account will not be taxed. That portion of your account will remain tax-free in either scenario.

Which Should You Choose?

I'll come right out and say it: I strongly urge you to save tax-free. That means paying your taxes now and accumulating your assets tax-free.

I have moved both of my children from tax-deferred to tax-free savings approaches. I have helped hundreds of savers do the same.

Why do I feel so strongly about this?

Two powerful reasons.

No. 1: Myth of the Lower Tax Rate in Retirement

First, because the myth of deferring taxes is just that: a myth.

Here's how the myth goes: You should defer taxes now and pay them later. While you're working, you're in a high tax bracket. When you retire, you'll be in a lower tax bracket, so it's better to pay those taxes later.

I'm about the take a blow torch to this myth, which has plagued so many savers.

First, the vast majority of my clients are not likely to be in a lower tax bracket in retirement. And there's a simple reason.

Think about the things you enjoy doing with your income. Going out to dinner. Living in a comfortable home. Traveling. Buying a new car every few years.

Are you willing to give up those things in retirement?

Most of us aren't. And that's where the myth of the lower tax bracket in retirement starts to get exposed. Many of us want the same luxuries in retirement we have pre-retirement. That means we're going to need approximately the same amount of income.

I came to discover the lower-tax-rate-in-retirement myth in a very personal way.

When I started deferring taxes on my 401(k), I was making $50,000 a year as an actuary at an insurance company called Capital

Holding. Today, as a successful actuary and business owner, I make quite a bit more. My tax bracket in 1980 was several levels lower than what it is today. But I still deferred those taxes at a lower rate. Now I have to pay a much higher rate when I spend my money. This is a very common challenge for successful professionals.

Today, I can see retirement on the horizon ahead. And I've done the math. I've worked out the income my wife and I will need to live the life we envision when I retire. And guess what? It's only about 5–10 percent less than what I make today. So my tax rate isn't going to be lower when I retire than it is now. And it certainly isn't going to be lower than when I was deferring all those taxes making $50,000 a year.

If you have a successful career and increase your income between now and retirement, the same could be true for you.

You don't have to take my word for it.

When Does It Make Sense?

You've probably heard of T. Rowe Price, a popular investment firm. The company recently did some research I found very powerful: it helped analyze the risk of saving tax-free vs. tax-deferred.

Let me give you the headline from the study, and then we'll work backward to how they arrived at it. Here it is: "When it comes to retirement, *nearly everyone under the age of fifty is better off saving tax-free rather than tax-deferred.*"

If that doesn't sound earth-shattering to you, consider this: if you're currently saving in a tax-deferred account (like a 401(k) or IRA), you could be giving up double-digit percentages of retirement income using that approach, according to the study.

All right, so what exactly did the T. Rowe Price study find? Check out the chart from the study. It tracks the same hypothetical savings pattern through various ages and tax scenarios to determine whether a tax-deferred plan (IRA) or a tax-free plan (Roth IRA) would provide more income in retirement. As you can tell, the tax-free savings approach wins nearly all of the time.

SAVING IN A ROTH 401(K) AT AGE 45 BEATS
SAVING IN A REGULAR 401(K) NO MATTER
WHAT HAPPENS TO YOUR TAXES IN 20 YEARS:

BOOST TO RETIREMENT INCOME IN A ROTH

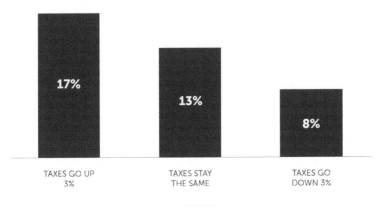

TAXES GO UP 3%	TAXES STAY THE SAME	TAXES GO DOWN 3%
17%	13%	8%

SOURCE:
T. Rowe Price Assumptions: Annualized 7% returns / 6% in retirement, retirement at age 65, withdrawals over 30 years, tax savings from pretax account invested in taxable account.

How much more spendable income can a Roth IRA offer over a traditional IRA?

AGE

		25	30	35	40	45	50	55
CHANGE IN TAX RATE	10%	35%	34%	32%	31%	29%	27%	25%
	5%	26%	25%	23%	22%	20%	19%	17%
	1%	19%	18%	17%	15%	14%	12%	11%
	0%	18%	17%	15%	14%	13%	11%	9%
	-1%	16%	15%	14%	12%	11%	10%	8%
	-5%	11%	9%	8%	7%	6%	4%	3%
	-10%	4%	3%	2%	1%	0%	-2%	10%

Roth does better   Neutral   Traditional does better

SOURCE:
T. Rowe Price. Assumes investor retired at age 65 and contributed $1,000 into a Roth IRA or a traditional IRA at various ages. Investor is in a 25% tax bracket at the time of contributions. The tax deduction is invested in a separate taxable account. An annualized 7% return is assumed for all accounts during working years, and a 6% rate is assumed for retirement years. A 25% tax is subtracted from the taxable account annually during the years leading up to retirement and taxed at the same rate as the income during retirement. Withdrawals were made over a 30-year retirement.

This study shows even if your tax rate *did* drop in retirement, most savers are still better off paying their taxes upfront and saving tax-free. Why? To answer that, we'll look at the next reason I am so committed to tax-free saving.

No. 2: Taxing the Seed vs. Taxing the Harvest

How your savings should be taxed isn't just a question of your tax rate now versus in the future. Let's say you think you'll be in a lower tax bracket when you retire. There is still an important reason you should save tax-free.

Under tax-deferred plans, all the earnings in your account will be taxed at a future rate. It's important to remember: you're not trying to live off your contributions alone in retirement. You probably can't save enough money to live off it comfortably. To retire, you're going to need your savings to GROW. If you're saving tax-deferred, all of that growth is going to be taxed.

Think about it like a garden. Under a tax-deferred plan, the seeds are planted tax-free, but the entire harvest is taxed. Under a plan that pays taxes upfront, the opposite is true. You're paying taxes on the seeds, but when it's time to harvest, all of that grain is yours, tax-free.

TAX-DEFERRED GROWTH
NOT TAXED
TAXED

TAX-FREE GROWTH
TAXED
NOT TAXED

Show Me the Numbers!

Well, I'm an actuary, so I like to substitute numbers for opinions. I don't need to *tell* you to save tax-free: I can *show* you.

Lots of people ask me if this is the best strategy, and I'm a little embarrassed to admit that until recently I had never put pen to paper and proven it. So, earlier this year, I sat down and did the math. I was amazed at what I discovered.

In a tax-deferred account, the growth is all going to be taxed when you withdraw it. So, you have to consider your overall tax liability on the account, not just how the money is taxed when contributed.

Sounds good in theory, but what do the numbers look like?

I used a client, thirty-five-year-old Paul, for this experiment. Paul pays about 33 percent of his income in taxes when you add up his federal, local and state tax obligations. He's contributing $7,500 annually to a tax-deferred account. For the purpose of this exercise, I assume he'll keep contributing to his account for thirty years until he's sixty-five. I also assume a 7 percent net annual growth rate, meaning his retirement account is growing 7 percent a year after fees. I assume he stays in the same tax bracket in retirement, as most of my clients do. We want to see the amount of taxes he avoided paying in his working years through deferral and how much he might have to pay when accessing the money in retirement.

Here are the raw numbers:

Tax Burden in a Tax-Deferred Account

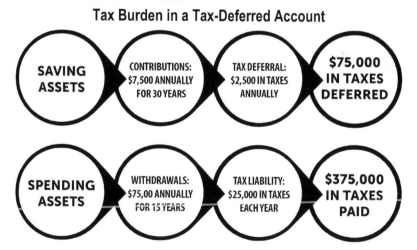

For this example, we've assumed an individual in the 33% tax bracket contributes $7,500 annually for 30 years with a 7% net annual growth rate into a tax-deferred asset, like a 401(k) or IRA. This hypothetical example does not consider every product feature of tax-deferred accounts and is for illustrative purposes only. It should not be deemed a representation of past or future results, and is no guarantee of return or future performance. This information is not intended to provide tax, legal or investment advice. Be sure to speak with qualified professionals before making any decisions about your personal situation.

Look at those right-hand circles. They should blow you away. They sure blew me away!

Paul is deferring **$75,000** in taxes over his working years. This is the big savings all of us are being promised with 401(k)s. After all, look at how much of his taxes he is able to avoid while working: $75,000!

Here's the catch, and it's a big catch. When Paul goes to spend his money in retirement, he owes **$375,000** in taxes. Remember, he deferred taxes on contributions only, but he's being taxed on his contributions and account growth. That makes poor Paul pay $300,000 extra dollars in taxes!

Of course, Paul could take his $75,000 of tax deferral during his working years, invest it in a fully taxable account until age sixty-five. Then he could use the growth (after taxes) of this fund to offset the extra taxes he incurs during his retirement years. Theoretically possible, but complex and not very realistic. After all, do you know anyone who actually does this? Of the thousands of savers I've met with, fewer than five are taking this approach. More likely, people take their tax deferral (in the form of a tax refund) and simply spend it. So they are faced with this big tax bill in their retirement years with no way to cover it other than their retirement income.

It's a pretty shocking analysis for most of our clients. But it's just the math associated with growing assets tax-deferred. When the principal AND growth have to be taxed in the future, it can really add up.

Now You're in the Know

Very few people have done what you just took the time to do: quantify their tax risk in traditional tax-deferred retirement plans. More smart, financially sophisticated savers make this mistake than any other.

And now you'll know better.

So, Fix It Already

I admit, the first New Rule of Retirement Saving has included a lot of doom and gloom. I've told you you're not saving enough, you're saving in the wrong vehicles, the stock market won't help you, but there's nowhere else to put your money. And now, on top of it all, you're going to owe gobs of taxes.

Clearly, actuaries don't make good inspirational speakers!

Don't despair. In the next section of this book, I'm going to show you a way you can eliminate all of these risks. Because the second New Rule of Retirement Saving is all about choosing strategies that address each of these risks.

CHAPTER SIX

RULE #2: Choose a Strategy That Addresses Your Risks

"Fortune favors the prepared mind." ~ Louis Pasteur

I started this book with a simple sentence: I did it wrong.

I'll start this chapter with a simple promise: you don't have to.

If there's one thing I've learned by being an actuary, it's that the real risks are the ones you don't know about, and therefore can't plan for. Risks that you can identify, you can often eliminate, or at least proactively address. That's what the rest of this book will teach you to do.

It's a little like boxing. The punches you see coming don't knock you out. You can prepare for those. It's the punch you didn't see coming that puts you on the mat.

In section one, we identified the punches coming your way: risks in how you save, the stock market and taxes. Now, I'm going to show you how to slip those punches like Muhammad Ali.

First, a quick summary. Our first New Rule of Retirement Saving was Know Your Risks. So far, we've identified three potential risks in your savings strategy:

Structural risk: What vehicle are you using to save? What features and benefits does that vehicle have? Is your company helping you save? Can you count on the government for support in your retirement?

Market risk: Will the market return enough for you to grow your retirement account? Will you lose money every time the market crashes? If you choose a safer savings vehicle, will you get any growth on your money at all?

Tax risk: Will your taxes be higher or lower in the future? Will you need to pay taxes on all the growth in your retirement account? How will taxes impact the dollar amount of income you'll be able to spend in retirement?

With our second New Rule of Retirement Saving, we are going to look for strategies that overcome all three of these risks.

But first, I want to introduce you to my daughter, Rebecca.

My Daughter

Meet my oldest daughter, Rebecca.

Her talent is political communication. Do you ever see congressmen and senators talking on Fox News about the issues of the day? Rebecca writes those talking points.

My daughter inherited many things from me, including my stubbornness and inquisitive mind. One thing she did not inherit was my financial sense.

About three years ago, Rebecca came to me with a question: she was switching jobs and didn't know what to do about her 401(k). Like a good saver, she had been putting money away for retirement since her first paycheck. She was now thirty-five. Unfortunately, her new job didn't offer a match, and she wasn't sure how much to save or what to do.

There were two main questions she had, and they should be the same questions you are asking yourself right now: How much do I need to save? And, what vehicle should I use to save it?

Over several hours, I went through an exercise with her to answer these two questions. In much less time than that, I'll go through the exercise with you as well.

Building Your Stool

Remember the three-legged stool from Chapter Three? Your grandparents and maybe even your parents had it.

Their retirement savings was made up of (1) employer contributions (through a pension or very high 401(k) match); (2) government contributions (through Social Security) and (3) personal contributions (through their personal savings).

As previously discussed, you will most likely have a one-legged stool, and that's hard to keep balanced. Unless you're a teacher or firefighter, you probably don't have a pension. Most of us don't have a high — if any — employer match to our 401(k). So the employer contribution leg is gone, or at least structurally weakened. And the demographics for Social Security don't look good. If you are under the age of fifty, there's a very real chance that Social Security as we know it today won't be around when you're ready to retire. So the government contribution leg isn't too strong either.

That leaves your personal savings leg. The rest of this chapter is about how to build a personal savings leg that is strong enough to hold up your entire retirement income needs.

Sound unbelievable? I promise there's a way.

How Much Should I Save?

There's a rule of thumb you might have heard: save 10 percent of your income for retirement. If you make $80,000 a year that means you should be saving $8,000 a year.

But here's a secret most people don't know: 10 percent a year is based on an employer match. Experts really advise that you save 15 percent a year of your salary. They're just assuming that 5 percent of your savings is coming from your employer.

If you have an employer matching 5 percent or more, by all means save 10 percent of your salary. But if you're like the majority of savers with no or low corporate match, then you really need to be saving closer to 15 percent.

I know, it hurts. But here's the thing: you can take out loans to buy a car. You can take out loans to send your children to college. But no one — no one — is going to lend you money to live on in retirement. That means you have to save today.

If you'd like something to help you determine how much you'll need at retirement, I've included a few charts in the addendum of this book. Feel free to take a moment and fill them out. This is especially helpful for savers in their twenties, thirties, and forties who still have a lot of saving years ahead of them.

Once you've figured out how much you need to save (or, if you're closer to retirement, once you've added up how much you've already saved), it's time to ask: How are you going to save it? To answer that, we return to your structural risk.

CHAPTER SEVEN

Choosing How You Save

"There are three constants in life: change, choice, and principles." ~ Stephen Covey

The single biggest decision you'll make when it comes to saving for your future is the decision to save. After that, the biggest choice you have is how you're going to save.

You might remember some of the shortcomings we discussed about the most common ways to save, namely traditional 401(k)s and IRAs, which accumulate tax-deferred; and Roth 401(k)s and IRAs, which accumulate tax-free.

Do you remember how I started this book? Go back and read the first sentence of Chapter One. Go ahead. I'll wait.

That's right: I did it wrong.

This entire book grew out of my frustration at saving the wrong way in my 401(k) and my desire to help people like you avoid those same mistakes.

There are many, many ways you can save for the future. You already know about some of them: 401(k)s and Roth IRAs. Or maybe you've never given them much thought at all and just saved in whatever your company offered. Maybe you've never saved for retirement at all.

But even with the most common types of retirement savings, knowing what your money and growth might look like years down the road makes a difference when you are considering how you're going to save.

Think back to the difference in the tax accumulation of traditional retirement accounts and their Roth counterparts:

	401(k)	Roth 401(k)
Taxes Paid	Deferred	Upfront
Growth	Many options, typically mutual funds; account value can go down	Many options, typically mutual funds; account value can go down
Penalties	10% tax penalty on all funds withdrawn before 59 ½	10% tax penalty on earnings only if funds withdrawn before 59 ½
Mandatory withdrawals	Yes, 70 ½	No
Contribution limits	Yes	Yes
Expenses/ fees	1–2% annually	1–2% annually

I can't tell you which approach is right for you. You're reading a book. I don't know you. I don't know your needs, your goals for the future, or your individual situation.

But I can tell you what I recommend to two of the most important people in my life: my daughters.

My daughters are currently thirty-nine (Rebecca — you met her before) and thirty-six (Sara). Both have found their way into good careers in marketing, and both are married: one to an engineer, and one to an attorney. I've been blessed with four grandchildren. Life is good.

Several years ago, I noticed something alarming. Both of my children were making the same mistakes I made. Both were saving for retirement in ways that exposed them to all the risks in this book.

And I hated it.

Every parent wants better for their children than they have for themselves, and that includes retirement. I didn't want my kids to reach sixty-five and think, "My IRA is just a big tax liability."

Being an actuary, I started analyzing different savings approaches and vehicles, trying to see what offered the best balance of growth, security, and tax advantages. It took me several months.

Then, one spring morning, as you'll remember from earlier, my oldest daughter Rebecca came to my office to ask for help.

First, I helped her figure out how much she should be saving.

Then, we had to address the question: What should she be saving it in?

Well, all my research and analysis had paid off. I had something exciting to show her.

Defining Success

When I was earning my Master of Business Administration degree back in the 1980s, a popular notion was "defining success." This was the process of answering one simple question: What does our experience look like if we're successful in what we're trying to achieve?

So I asked Rebecca to define success for her retirement savings account. What benefits would an ideal strategy deliver?

Together, we wrote out a list of everything an ideal retirement savings plan would have. She added some items, and I added some items. Here's what we came up with.

For my retirement plan,
I want:

1. Growth
2. Security
3. No high fees
4. Flexible
5. Lowest amount of tax

The money needs to grow. The account has to get bigger and bigger as the years go on. It has to get big enough that I can fund my entire retirement from it.

The money needs to be safe. When the market drops or our economy stumbles, the account shouldn't suffer. Anytime I want to retire, the money — all of the money — should be there for me.

It needs to be flexible. Sometimes there are good reasons to take funds out before retirement. Sometimes there are good reasons to put extra funds in. I just don't want all these IRS strings attached to it.

It needs to grow tax-free. I don't want to pay taxes on all the earnings in the account.

It needs to be low-cost. I hate paying expensive fees.

It's a good list. No, it's a *great* list, and it overcomes all the risks we've outlined in this book:

- Growth and protection overcome market volatility
- Tax-free overcomes the tax risk
- Flexibility and low fees overcome the structural risk

So I shared my research with her. Together, we looked at each common way to save for retirement to see if it could achieve **all** these goals.

	401(k)/ IRA	Roth 401(k)/ IRA	Savings Account	Money Market Fund
Meaningful growth	X	X		
Protection from bad markets			X	X
Tax-free income		X		
Flexibility				X
Low fees			X	X

Unfortunately, none of them could achieve all her goals. But I had something else in mind.

This is a very special part of the book, because I'm about to share with you one of the most exciting developments in retirement savings this century.

Before we start, I want to tell you something important. I don't know your individual situation. I want to share with you what I am doing for my own two daughters when it comes to their retirement savings, and what I've helped hundreds of people like you do for themselves. Only you can decide if this approach is valuable to you and your situation.

You're Looking in the Wrong Part of the Tax Code

Have you ever wondered where the 401(k) got its name?

It's named after a section of the U.S. tax code. Section 401, subsection k, enables individuals to save funds for retirement, with certain restrictions, tax-deferred.

It's a funny realization. In truth, 401(k)s are just savings vehicles that utilize certain portions of our national tax code. Basically, they're shopping carts. You can load up mutual funds, bonds, and other savings instruments into your 401(k) shopping cart and they'll receive a particular tax status.

Section 401, subsection k, is not the only part of the tax code that delivers tax benefits to a savings approach. In fact, there are many parts of the tax code you can save under for the future.

In this book, I want to introduce you to Section 7702.

7702 Plans

Meet section 7702 of the Internal Revenue Code.

Section 7702 has been available for saving for years. In fact, it well predates section 401(k). Only recently has its use become more widespread, as people like you have realized the large deficiencies in section 401(k).

Here's what a properly structured 7702 plan can deliver:

(1) Growth when the market is up

(2) Protection when the market drops

(3) Tax-free savings growth

(4) Low cost

(5) Flexibility to contribute and access funds without restrictions

It sounds great, right?

But what exactly is a 7702 plan?

Life Insurance. Yes, Life Insurance.

Wait, don't close the book!

I know "life insurance" isn't what you expected to see as a solution to your retirement savings problems. Frankly, I didn't expect it either. In fact, I almost wrote it off. But as an actuary who has made his career in the insurance industry, I knew the benefits of life insurance. And I knew certain kinds of life insurance were flexible enough to possibly deliver all the benefits my daughter had on her list.

So I set off to see what I could use my actuarial skills to structure. What I discovered is changing the savings industry.

First, let's talk about life insurance. The number 7702 refers to the part of the U.S. tax code that enables funds inside a life insurance policy to accumulate (or grow) tax-free, and provide a death benefit to heirs tax-free.

Saying life insurance is good for saving is like saying stocks are good for saving. There are too many different kinds, features and benefits to paint with a brush that broad. Some are clearly better than others.

I assume you're not an actuary. So you probably don't want to evaluate every kind of insurance on the market and determine the best one for saving.

Thankfully, I am an actuary, and I've done it for you. Here's the deal.

IUL

IUL. These three little letters just may change the entire way you save for the future.

Section 7702 existed for years before people really started taking advantage of it. Why? Because while the tax code allowed individuals to save in life insurance policies, the life insurance products on the market weren't very good for saving.

That all started to change in the early 1990s, with a new breed of life insurance products designed specifically to help people like you save and grow their funds while also getting death protection.

That revolution was IUL.

IUL stands for **indexed universal life**, a very flexible form of life insurance that is often used as a savings vehicle, as well as for death protection.

As I picked apart an IUL policy to understand how it could be used for savings, I discovered I could check off all the priorities on my daughter's list of retirement savings goals. That's because IUL delivers three benefits that no other savings vehicle does:

- Tax-free income in retirement
- The power of indexing to grow your funds
- A death benefit to make your plan self-completing

We'll look at each of these benefits in depth over the next few chapters.

Be Your Own Detective

One thing I encourage my clients to do is be their own detective. That means asking lots of questions that drill down to one answer: Does what I'm hearing bring value to me?

Now, it's a little hard to raise your hand and ask a question while reading a book. But I know you're smart, and I know you want to do the right thing for your future. Otherwise, why would you be reading a book on saving?

So as I walk you through the benefits of this savings approach, take a moment to see if they solve some of the risks in your own savings plan. I think you'll be surprised.

CHAPTER EIGHT

Eliminating Structural Risk

First, let's look at how IUL can address your structural risks. Remember that checklist my daughter and I created? The one that shows what an ideal retirement savings strategy should have?

Let's add IUL to the mix and see how it performs.

	401(k)/ IRA	Roth 401(k)/ IRA	Savings Account	Money Market Fund	Indexed Universal Life (IUL)
Meaningful growth	X	X			X
Protection from bad markets			X	X	X
Tax-free income		X			X
Flexibility				X	X
Low fees			X	X	X

Pretty amazing, right?

That's what I thought. My daughter, Rebecca, wanted to know more. "How on earth can it do all those things?" she wanted to know.

Let's explore that question.

Gaining Flexibility

Here's an ugly truth: In your 401(k) or IRA, the IRS is calling all the shots.

The IRS has decided you can retire at age fifty-nine-and-one-half. But sometimes you need to access your retirement funds before that date. What if you want to use some of these funds to send your child to college, or cover a medical emergency?

Well, in a 401(k) or IRA, you pay a hefty price. Not only do you pay taxes on the money you withdraw, you pay an extra 10-percent tax penalty. If your taxes are around 25 percent, that means you'll give 35 percent of your money to the IRS if you need your funds early.

Now let's look at the flip side. The IRS wants to collect the taxes on the funds in your 401(k) or IRA. So the government requires you to take money out of your fund at age seventy-and-one-half. What if you're still working and don't need the income? Too bad. You have to take it (and pay taxes on it) anyway.

With IUL, it's different. Properly structured, you can access funds anytime you want. Need to use a little of your savings to send your kids to college? Fine. Want to put that money back into your account few years later? Great. Are you seventy-two and still using other assets for retirement? Fine, leave the money in your IUL policy until you need it. No big deal.

A Self-Completing Plan

Flexibility isn't the only benefit of choosing an IUL structure to save for retirement. These plans are also self-completing, and that was an important consideration for my daughter.

Here's the great thing about IUL: it's life insurance.

And life insurance comes with a death benefit.

Now, maybe you have kids and that death benefit is important. Maybe you plan to have kids in the future. Maybe you have a spouse you want to protect.

A death benefit makes your retirement savings plan self-completing.

What does self-completing mean?

David and Janie, both age forty-one, are my clients. David earns the majority of their income, with Janie holding a part-time job as a preschool aide. Needless to say, most of the money they put away for retirement comes from David's paycheck.

Both David and Janie will need income to live on in retirement. So what happens if, heaven forbid, David were to get hit by a car crossing the street today and not survive?

Janie will still need retirement income, but now the paycheck that delivers their savings money — David's — is gone.

The fact of the matter is, 401(k)s are just not self-completing. If you die, your 401(k) is worth whatever is in your 401(k) on that day. Oh, and taxes are still due. So make that 20 to 30 percent **less** than what was in your 401(k) on that day.

Thankfully, Janie and David aren't saving for retirement in a 401(k). They're using IUL. So if David gets hit by that car, Janie won't just have the account value of what they've saved. She'll have a death benefit that will make up for all the future contributions David is no longer able to make. Her lifetime savings won't suffer. Her retirement won't be at risk.

As you can see, IUL overcomes many of the structural risks you face when saving in other popular vehicles. But what about the other risks? Flexibility isn't enough. You need your money to grow, too.

CHAPTER NINE

Eliminating Market Risk

"I don't know anything about the stock market. And I stay away from things I don't know anything about." ~ *Wayne Gretzky*

The biggest problem with 401(k)s and IRAs is that growth is often dependent on the stock market. As we've seen, the market can rise and fall, creating an unsteady environment in which to grow your funds. In most savings vehicles, when the market is up you make money and when the market crashes you lose money. It's a boom and bust cycle.

IUL overcomes this through indexing.

The "indexed" in indexed universal life explains how interest is credited to a policy. This technique lets you grow your money when the market is up, but protects your money when the market drops. It's a "best of both worlds" approach. What's even better? It's pretty simple to understand.

In indexing, you capture a portion of the stock market's growth, up to a cap. As of this writing, those caps tend to be around 11-12 percent. So if the market goes up 10 percent next year, you would get 10 percent growth in your policy. If the market goes up 15 percent, you would get the cap of 11.5 percent, for example.

Here's the special magic: your account has a floor of zero. This means the least amount of interest you can be credited in a year is zero percent. If the market drops 15 percent this year, your account receives no interest . . . but it doesn't lose any value, either. It just stays where it is.

In the following chart, the bottom line represents $100,000 invested in the S&P 500®, including dividends — the most common measure of the stock market, as you may remember. This is the same line we examined earlier in the book. As you can see, after the tech bubble burst in 2000, the market dropped for three straight years. It built back up through the middle of the decade and then dropped again with the real estate bubble burst. At the end of last year, after eighteen years in the market, your $100,000 grew to $246,507, for an average total return of 4.8 percent a year.

We've already discussed the problems you face when only earning an average of 4.8 percent on your savings (minus fees and taxes, that's just not enough growth for the retirement income you'll likely want in the future).

Now, let's do a comparison and see how indexing performed during this same time period.

The Power of Indexing

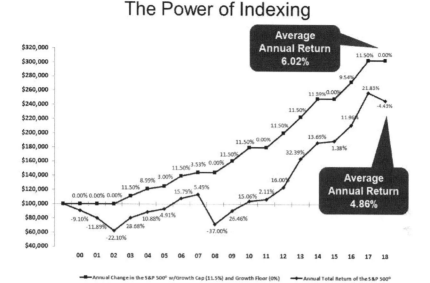

The top line of the chart represents the concept of indexing inside an IUL policy.[16] Look at the difference in growth. You can see that by eliminating the down years of the market, your account never loses value, and, therefore, can grow money much more efficiently.

As you can see, when the market is crashing from 2000 to 2003, the IUL policy is credited zero percent. Those are some of the happiest years because everything else is losing money while you're holding your own. In 2003, when the market turns around, the indexed policy begins net-positive growth immediately. It doesn't have to dig out of the hole from where the market dropped. Again in 2008, the policy is credited zero percent, and the next year immediately beings net-positive growth again.

---

[16] The indexed example utilizes a hypothetical index with a cap of 11.5 percent and a floor of zero percent.

So at the end of eighteen years, the $100,000 inside the index has grown to $303,845. That means the total average amount of interest credited to your account is 6.02 percent a year.

Let's look at an even scarier market. Some call the first decade of this century — from 2000 to 2009 — "the lost decade" as far as net growth in the American stock market is concerned. To say it was a very poor market is an understatement. It encompasses the market crashes of 2000 and 2008, as well as some of the market recovery.

Remember, during this decade, the S&P 500® (including dividends) returned an average of -1 percent a year. That's right. Money invested in the market LOST 1 percent a year. No wonder 2000 to 2009 has earned the title of worst decade in the history of the S&P 500®.

Indexing in the "Worst Decade"

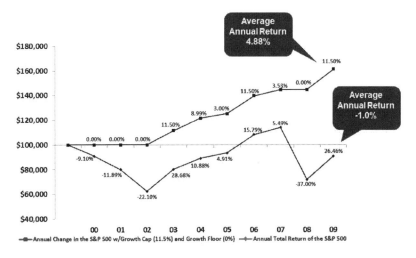

Indexing performed much better. By eliminating just a few bad (negative) years (2000 to 2002 and 2008) and making them zero percent credited interest, the index had an average annual credited rate of 4.8 percent. That's not too shabby in a market that is losing money!

Indexing lets you capture a good portion of the upside, with no downside risk. Once that interest is credited to your account, you never give it back, even if the market drops. As a result, it creates a return pattern that is incredibly powerful.

This is one powerful way you can eliminate market risk in your retirement savings. With indexing, it doesn't matter when you want to retire: when the market is strong, your account is growing. When the market is down, your account value stays strong. It doesn't matter if the market rises and falls because you don't have to earn back market losses, like in a 401(k) with mutual funds. Indexing delivers a steady, predictable growth pattern that slashes your market risk.

What's the Worst That Can Happen?

I know indexing is powerful, but my daughter, Rebecca, wanted more proof.

So I asked her a simple question: What is the scariest economic period in U.S. history?

I bet her answer is the same one you're thinking of now: the Great Depression.

We've all heard tales of the wild market swings that took place throughout the 1930s. It was a truly unprecedented time.

So I wanted to show Rebecca how the Great Depression would have turned out for someone in an IUL policy. How would this strategy fare in one of the most turbulent economies our country has ever known?

First, let's look at what the stock market did during the Great Depression and the ensuing recovery.

Today, the S&P 500®, that measurement we've discussed of the 500 largest stocks, is the standard-bearer for how we measure a market's strength or weakness. Of course, in 1929, analysts didn't measure the top 500 stocks. Thankfully, academics have gone back and calculated how the top 500 stocks in the market performed in the 1920s and 30s. Here's how those stocks performed:

HISTORICAL TOTAL RETURNS
(INCLUDING DIVIDENDS)
OF THE 500 LARGEST STOCKS:

YEAR	PERFORMANCE
1929	-8.3
1930	-25.1
1931	-43.8
1932	-8.6
1933	+50.0
1934	-1.2
1935	+46.7
1936	+31.9
1937	-35.3
1938	+29.3

SOURCE: http://www.stern.nyu.edu/~adamore/New_Home_Page/data.html

So what happened to someone who, in 1929, had $100 invested in the stock market? Five years after the Great Depression started, his $100 has been reduced to $53. He lost 47 percent of his money.

Miraculously, after eight years, he'd be back to a little above break-even. The market has rallied and in 1937 he finally had more money than he started with.

Then the market crashed again. At the end of 1938, he'd have $84.64 in his pocket. What a decade!

Put another way, $100 invested in the stock market at the beginning of 1929 was worth about $35 by 1932. Despite the recovery that followed, by the end of the decade in 1938, your $100 investment was worth about $85.

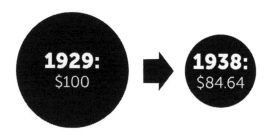

So what would an indexed insurance product have looked like during the Great Depression? First, some assumptions. Let's give this index the range of a common IUL product in the market today — a floor of zero percent and a ceiling of 11.5 percent. Secondly, we'll continue using those same back-projected estimates of the S&P 500®, since that measurement didn't exist in the 1930s.

Here's what indexing looked like in the Great Depression:

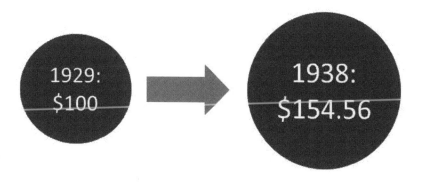

Pretty amazing, right? The $100 in our hypothetical index would be worth $154.56 by 1938. That's a growth rate of 4.45 percent a year . . . during the GREAT DEPRESSION!

How is this possible? It all comes down to math. When you eliminate any negative years *and* you never give back the interest you've accumulated, it's easier to realize net-positive gains over the long run. So during the Great Depression, everyone else was losing their wealth when the market dropped. But you, with your indexed account, just got zero percent interest that year. No big deal. And the next year, you started growing again from a positive position.

This is why I love the concept of indexing.

What do others say?

The Money Manager

I have a client by the name of Will, who is one of the smartest financial guys I know. Before he retired, he managed billions of dollars in institutional pension funds. Essentially, it was his job to grow enough money for a company to pay everyone their pension.

Indexing piqued his interest. But, of course, he wanted to run his own analysis on it.

So he back-tested indexing in numerous historical periods. How would it perform when the market was down, up or on a roller-coaster ride? What about in times of slow growth? Fast growth?

When we sat down one January afternoon, he set a ream of paper on the table, heavy enough to make a "thud." This was his analysis. I asked him what he had determined, and here's what he told me:

"Marty, the return pattern in this product is so unique, it's unlike anything else in my portfolio. I think everyone should own an asset like this."

Translation into non-money-manager speak? The balance of protection and growth is unlike anything else. Everyone needs to take advantage.

Pretty high praise from a guy who was used to working with the stock market.

Now you see why.

CHAPTER TEN

Eliminating Tax Risk

"The avoidance of taxes is the only intellectual pursuit that still carries any   reward."
~ John Maynard Keynes

L et's think back to the tax chapter. As you remember, there are two kinds of savings approaches:

- **Tax-deferred**, which means you do not pay taxes on your contributions today, but you pay taxes on your contributions and all the earnings in your account when you get the money in retirement. This is your typical 401(k) or IRA.
- **Tax-free**, which means you pay taxes now on your contributions, but then they grow tax-free. When you go to retire, you don't owe any taxes on the money when you receive it. This is how Roth IRAs work, and also how IUL works.

Properly structured, you can access funds from an IUL policy completely tax-free. That's what Section 7702 of the U.S. Tax Code allows. The funds you grow in your policy can be used with no tax due.

You remember this example about my client, Paul?

Tax Burden in a Tax-Deferred Account

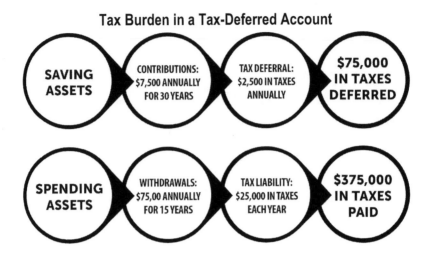

For this example, we've assumed an individual in the 33% tax bracket contributes $7,500 annually for 30 years with a 7% net annual growth rate into a tax-deferred asset, like a 401(k) or IRA. This hypothetical example does not consider every product feature of tax-deferred accounts and is for illustrative purposes only. It should not be deemed a representation of past or future results, and is no guarantee of return or future performance. This information is not intended to provide tax, legal or investment advice. Be sure to speak with qualified professionals before making any decisions about your personal situation.

Paul is planning to defer $75,000 in taxes over his working years, and he felt great about it! He loved not paying those taxes today, while he was saving.

As we now know, this doesn't work out so well for Paul. Why? Because in retirement, Paul owes $375,000 in taxes!

Properly structured IUL can help you avoid being like Paul. You're going to have to pay taxes one way or another on the money you put into your savings account. Uncle Sam isn't going to let you have it for free.

I'm betting paying $75,000 sounds a lot better to you than paying $375,000.

IUL can deliver this.

There are additional tax advantages with IUL, too. These were pretty important to my daughter Rebecca, as well.

In all life insurance, the death benefit is paid to heirs completely income-tax-free. That means if Rebecca were to die prematurely, her entire death benefit would be passed to her husband and children without any taxes due.

Remember when we talked about a self-completing plan? It's good to know that should something happen and you not make it to retirement, your heirs will get their full benefit — and not lose a penny of it to Uncle Sam.

Brief and to the Point

This is a pretty short chapter. I know I don't have to sell you on the benefits of saving tax-free rather than tax-deferred. We took care of that in Chapter Five.

So I'll just say this: protecting against risk is all about protecting against the worst-case scenario. When saving for retirement, the worst case is paying more in taxes than you have to. IUL is a sterling way to eliminate as much of your tax risk as possible.

Accomplishing Rule # 2

Remember the second New Rule of Retirement Saving: Choose a Strategy That Addresses Your Risks.

In the past few chapters, we've talked about eliminating structural risk with a plan that's flexible and self-completing. We've talked about eliminating market risk, through the power of indexing. And we've talked about eliminating tax risk through tax-free income in retirement.

IUL can eliminate all this risk. It's pretty amazing, right?

Maybe . . . too amazing?

CHAPTER ELEVEN

Too Good to Be True

"Trust but verify." ~ Russian proverb

I've talked about IUL as a retirement savings approach to hundreds and hundreds of people like you. There's one question I get every time:

"This sounds too good to be true. What's the catch?"

The truth is, there isn't much of a catch. Like any financial decision, it's important to work with a qualified professional, and it's important to make sure the strategy meets your personal goals.

That's why I always encourage good due diligence from my clients. It's important to ask questions and feel like the answers put you at ease.

Here's the deal: you're smart. I know you're smart because people who aren't smart don't make it to Chapter Eleven in a book about saving.

What do smart people do when they hear about an idea that's new to them? They Google it.

I would, too.

Of course, there are detractors from any financial strategy.

So let's talk about the top concerns you find when you Google "using IUL for retirement savings."

Truthful Scale

As an actuary, I believe in dispelling myth with fact. So below I've outlined the most common objections to using IUL for retirement savings, and rated how truthful they are using the "Truthful Scale" below. One star means the objection is not truthful. The objection is likely based on misinformation or intended to misinform. Two stars means the objection has some truth to it, or it may be true in some situations. Three stars means the objection is truthful and you should pay attention to it.

Truthful Scale:

* Not truthful. Likely based on misinformation or intended to misdirect.

** Somewhat truthful. May be true in some situations.

*** Truthful. Evaluate this objection carefully.

Objection: Structure

"IUL is pretty complex, and if it's structured wrong, you could get a raw deal."

Truthful Scale: ***

IUL can be structured many ways, and not all of those structures deliver the most value to you. Always work with a highly qualified professional on your IUL policy. I worked for almost two months to develop the perfect structure for my daughters' plans, and it's a structure we now use with most of our clients. IUL must be structured properly to deliver all the benefits we've discussed in this book. If you need help finding someone reputable in your area who uses our structure, call our office and we can help you identify someone.

Objection: Unrealistic Proposals

"They're making IUL look better than it is by using unrealistic assumptions about future growth."

Truthful Scale: **

It's impossible to predict what any financial instrument will do in the future. So the best we can do is look at past performance and project that forward. It's true with IUL, and it's true with 401(k)s, IRAs, and most financial products. However, IUL has the power of indexing. If you remember from our discussion of indexing, it helps stabilize the growth of your funds, because there are no negative years to deal with. So while the market may be up 30 percent one year and down 40 percent the next, indexing is more stable and thus less susceptible to unrealistic assumptions than other financial products.

This is one of the reasons I always show my clients some "worst case" scenarios as well, and why in this book I wanted to show how indexing could perform in terrible markets, like the Great Depression and the first decade of this century.

To get a complete picture, talk to your advisor about the full range of returns that might be reasonable to assume you could receive. I'm glad that industry regulators have recently established new rules that should help prevent any advisors from showing projections that are too aggressive or unreasonable.

Objection: Expense

"Never use insurance to save for retirement. It's so expensive!"

Truthful Scale: *

Here's one of my favorite myths about IUL, because it's so easy to dispel. There's a common refrain: life insurance is too expensive to use as a savings tool. What this means is that life insurance contains fees.

So do 401(k)s.[17] And IRAs.[18] And Roth IRAs. So when people tell me, "IUL is too expensive," I always ask them, "Compared to what?"

Let's look at the fees you could pay in each kind of account.

401(k)	IRA	IUL
Administrative Fees – fees that pay the company administering your account	Advisor Fees – fees to the person managing your funds for managing your account	Mortality Fees – fees that support your life insurance death benefit
Management Fees – fees that pay for the management of assets in certain kinds of funds	Managed Account Fees – fees that pay for the creation of a portfolio within your account	Expense Fees – fees that support the expenses of establishing, underwriting and managing your account
Fund Fees – fees for the mutual funds or other funds held in your account	Fund Fees – fees for the mutual funds or other	

[17] U.S. Department of Labor. "A Look at 401(k) Plan Fees." http://www.dol.gov/ebsa/publications/401k_employee.html.

[18] Robert Powell. MarketWatch. Aug. 10, 2010. "No free lunches, no fee-free IRAs." http://www.marketwatch.com/story/no-free-lunches-no-fee-free-iras-2013-08-10.

	funds held in your account	

As you can see in the accompanying chart, there are a variety of fees in all products. Fees are how the companies providing these savings vehicles make money. Fees have to be an accepted part of your retirement savings plans.

But you don't want to pay more fees than necessary. The fact of the matter is, 401(k) and IRA fees can be very high. The average cost for a 401(k) plan with fewer than one hundred employees is 1.4 percent. For more than one hundred employees it's 1.03 percent.[19] That fee is charged on your funds every year as you're working and contributing money, and when you're retired and drawing down money.

If you are in a 401(k) plan, not only are you paying an administrator to manage the 401(k) plan itself, but every time you put money into a mutual fund you have an additional set of fees that you're paying. What do those fees buy you? Well, you get access to mutual funds, and maybe some investment advice.

In an IUL policy you pay a "cost of insurance" fee and "general expense" fees. For these fees, you get some real benefits: a death benefit, tax-free savings growth and, of course, *the power of indexing* to grow your funds over time.

Sure, you're thinking, you get a lot for those fees. But the fees are still so high!

That's What Neil Thought

Neil, a team member in my office, came to us from the world of managed money. His background is in investing, and he didn't trust

---

[19] Society for Human Resource Management. Feb. 28, 2013. "401(k) Plan Fees Declined — Slightly — in 2012." http://www.shrm.org/hrdisciplines/benefits/articles/pages/401k-feeseclined.aspx.

life insurance as a savings vehicle. Why, you might ask? He had always been told it was too expensive.

When he started working with us, he always came back to cost: "But how can we recommend something with such high fees?"

I wasn't convinced the fees were so high. Being an actuary, I decided to look at the numbers.

First, I wanted to compare apples to apples. In a managed account like an IRA or 401(k), fees tend to stay uniform as a percentage of assets throughout the life of the account. For example, you might owe 2 percent in fees on your account that currently has $100,000 in it. You would pay $2,000 in fees. You will likely owe that same 2 percent of fees in twenty years, when your account has grown to, say, $500,000. That year, you would owe $10,000 in fees. In an IUL policy, fees are structured differently. In these products, fees are typically front-loaded to pay a higher percentage on assets in early years, when the account balance is low. That means you're paying more fees when you have a little money, and dramatically less in fees when your account has grown. So, to compare fees in both products, I had to convert an IUL's fees into an annualized percentage, just like in a 401(k).

I took Neil, who is forty, and compared the fees he was paying in his 401(k) to the fees he'd pay in an IUL policy. Then we pitted the average annual fee from both strategies against each other.

What we discovered blew Neil away, and made him a true believer. I think it will blow you away, too.

The advisors Neil had been working with in his previous job usually charged their clients around 1 percent for their services. When added with mutual fund fees and other fees, their clients were paying 2 percent or more in portfolios that took pride in their "low-cost" nature.

How did IUL fare? In one IUL product I examined, Neil would be paying, on average, 0.76 percent of his annual account value in fees.

For half the cost of the average 401(k) and a third of the cost of the average advisor-managed account, Neil could access all the benefits of IUL.

The bottom line? When IUL is properly structured to also help you save, the policies can have very competitive costs and deliver a lot more for those fees, too.

In short, don't ever let anyone tell you that life insurance is too expensive a way to save.

Now you know better.

CHAPTER TWELVE

Rule #3: Take Action Now

"There is no happiness without action." ~ Benjamin Disraeli

W e've spent a lot of this book talking about your savings risks and how to identify those risks. You know what? If you're not saving, the risks don't matter.

You know it's important to save for your future. And you know it's important to save *enough* for your future.

So why is saving so unpleasant?

Many experts blame the lackluster economy. In recent years, you and your peers have saved through some of the worst economic times in history. Not one but two market crashes, persistently low interest rates and sluggish recoveries. It's enough to make anyone throw up their hands and quit.

For some of you, I think another factor is also to blame.

Retirement may be a long way away. If you're in your sixties, retirement is likely the center of your financial attention. But, if you're in your thirties or forties, retirement might seem like another lifetime. And even if you're in your fifties and can see retirement on the horizon, it's still not your most pressing concern. Paying your mortgage, financing college for your kids, paying off debt: those are your immediate needs. Finding the best way to save for retirement? You'll get to that soon. That thinking lets you put off making important decisions about how to save.

Maybe you're like my daughter, who was saving in a 401(k) because, well, it's what her company offered. You put money away but never really think about it. You just know it's the "right" thing to do.

All of this is to say: When something better comes along, it's hard to make a change. Saving for retirement isn't top of mind on a daily basis. You'll get around to making sure you're saving right later. Soon. When you find time.

Here's the danger with this mindset: it costs you real, significant income in retirement. Once you get to retirement, you can't go back and change the way you've been saving all these years. You have to make the decision to save — and save the right way — today.

Want to see why it matters?

Here's a Penny

I'm giving you a penny. It's not much — just a single penny. But let's say that penny doubles every day for a month. On Day Two, your penny is now two pennies. On Day Three, your penny is now four pennies. At the end of one month, how much money do you think you'd have? $20? $100?

Think again. As incredible as it may seem, at the end of thirty days, you, with your penny doubling every day, you will have more than *$10 million* — all from a single penny. That is the power of compound interest.

Encyclopedias attribute the following quote to Albert Einstein: "Compound interest is the eighth wonder of the world. He who understands it, earns it; he who doesn't, pays it." Compound interest is a powerful force in shaping our financial future. The sooner you start saving the right way, the sooner you can put compounding to work for you.

If Columbus Had Found a Penny . . .

In elementary school, we all learned the rhyme, "In 1492, Columbus sailed the ocean blue" to help us remember the date. Well, what if (and you have to use your imagination here) ol' Christopher had found a penny on the beaches of the New World. Instead of putting it in his pocket, he invested it in an account earning 6 percent interest. Let's say he found someone whom he could trust to carry out his instructions and told them to leave the penny in the account but take out the interest every year and put it in a piggy bank. By the 21st century, that piggy bank would have about thirty cents in it. No big deal, right?

But if Christopher Columbus had placed that penny in an account returning 6 percent compound interest, the account would be worth more than $121 billion today! You don't believe me? Okay. I discovered this illustration in 2009, which is 517 years from 1492. Go ahead, you can check my math. Your initial investment of one penny, each time it is compounded, will be 106 percent of its original value, right? So that 106 percent is taken times itself, or compounded, 517 times. Pull out your calculator and type in 1.06 multiplied by 1.06, 517 times. Then multiply that answer by 0.01, your penny, and you should come up with $121,096,709,346.21. Can you see now why Albert Einstein was so impressed with compound interest? Granted, you are unlikely to live 517 years to collect on a one-cent investment, but it makes the point that saving early can greatly increase your chance of success.

There have been scores of books written about compound interest, and a quick Google search will give you more reading material than perhaps you need. So I'll just say this: everything you put away today is pennies. Every day you defer putting those pennies away, you defer that amazing outcome.

My Daughter, the Procrastinator

My daughter, Rebecca, is very efficient. Every morning, she manages to get her kids up, dressed, fed, and out the door with everything they need for a day at school. At the same time, she gets herself ready for a day at the office, makes sure all the permission slips are filled out, all the bills are paid, and everyone (including her husband) has their lunch.

But there's one area where Rebecca is a bit of a procrastinator, and that's making big financial decisions.

After we met about IUL, Rebecca was pretty excited. But she was also busy. She was changing jobs, taking care of my grandchildren, repainting her kitchen, and serving as chair of *two* different community organizations.

So, she told me what many people tell me when it's time to act: "I really like this plan. Can we talk about it in a few months when things slow down?"

Now, because Rebecca is my daughter, I was blunt with her. And because you and I have been together for more than eleven chapters now, I'll be blunt with you, too: No, you cannot wait.

You have to start saving the right way, right now.

Rebecca is very practical. I knew if I could quantify how much she's giving up by putting off this decision, she'd come around.

So I ran some numbers and here's what I found.

Let's say you're forty-two years old and put off the decision to start saving the right way for five years. Do you know how much income you'll be giving up when you retire? Forty-two percent. That means every year in retirement, you'll have 42 percent less money to spend than if you had just started saving today.

But wait, Rebecca told me. "I'm not going to put it off for five years. Maybe just a few months or a year."

Okay. Here's the bad news. If you wait even just one year to start saving the right way, you'll have 10 percent less income to spend . . . every year of retirement.

Needless to say, Rebecca started the next week.

Regardless of what financial approach you take to saving for retirement, I hope you'll take action now. Don't give up 10 percent of your retirement. Saving benefits those who take action.

CHAPTER THIRTEEN

Final Thoughts

"To help, to continually help and share: that is the sum of all knowledge."
~ Eleanora Duse

I wrote this book because I did it wrong.

I wrote it so you, my kids, my colleagues, and people I don't know and might never meet, won't make the same mistakes.

You don't have to do it wrong. You can do it right.

Remember way at the beginning of the book when we thought about what life would look like at age seventy-five? Right now, sitting in your chair, reading this book, it's hard to imagine being seventy-five. It's hard to imagine having to rely on your savings for everything you need in life: food, housing, travel, clothes. Today, you have control: you can work harder, switch jobs, get additional education and make more money. In retirement, you cede control to the choices you've made in your past. Choices about how to save, how much to save and when to save. Choices you're making right now determine everything in retirement.

That's why I encourage you to be bold. To be a detective. To take an active role in planning your future rather than letting your future happen to you. To use the New Rules of Retirement Savings.

Fat-Free Frozen Yogurt

If you're a Seinfeld fan like me, you've undoubtedly taken more than a few life lessons from the TV show that's just supposed to make you laugh. But there's one episode that sticks out in my mind when I think about people mindlessly saving in their 401(k)s.

Do you remember the Seinfeld episode where Kramer invests in a fat-free frozen yogurt shop? It's the hot new hit in town, and George, Elaine and Jerry find themselves eating there almost daily. After all, the frozen yogurt is so flavorful, so delicious... and it's fat-free! There's no guilt in eating it.

A few weeks later, Jerry and Elaine are perplexed. None of their clothes fit. They've put on 7 or 8 pounds. They can't figure out what happened.

Until they remember the fat-free frozen yogurt.

No, says Kramer. It can't be the yogurt. The yogurt is fat-free. It's good for you.

As we all know, it *was* the yogurt. Because fat-free doesn't mean calorie-free. And it doesn't mean sugar-free.

So why does this remind me of saving for retirement?

401(k)s are the fat-free frozen yogurt of the savings industry. They have become the most popular way to save for retirement. People plow savings into them every day. And they feel good about it, because their money is growing tax-deferred. It's fat-free. It has benefits.

Of course, savers are overlooking the other features that matter when saving — the calories and sugar content, if you will. Is deferring your taxes helpful? What restrictions come with 401(k)s?

Much as it took weeks for Jerry and Elaine to discover the unsavory downside of yogurt (weight gain), most people don't realize the downside of their 401(k) until it's too late and they're nearing retirement. That's what happened to me, and if you talk to people in their sixties and seventies, there's a good chance it's what happened to them, too.

I want to steer you away from that fat-free frozen yogurt binge. I want to make sure the food you're eating today will sustain you for many years to come.

That's why I wrote this book.

I did it wrong.

Now, you don't have to.

Longevity Risk and How Much You Need to Retire

This book has focused on *how* you save: what savings approach can deliver the greatest success in growing your money and delivering valuable benefits.

There's an equally important question that often gets overlooked, and that's *how much* you should save. Because the best savings strategy in the world won't matter if you're not, you know, actually saving and saving enough.

In previous chapters, we've discussed the common advice to save around 10 percent of your income for retirement. How do you know if that will be enough?

It's one of the most common questions I hear, and one that doesn't have an easy answer. After all, there are many unknowns: When will you retire? How long will you live? How will the market perform during your savings years? How will it perform during your retirement years? What will be the rate of inflation? The list goes on and on.

You can't know if you're on the right track if you don't know where your track is going. So let's take a few moments to consider how long you might live in retirement, and how much you need to save to fund it.

Longevity Risk

This book has focused on the three main risks you face when saving for retirement: structural risk, market risk, and tax risk.

There's a fourth risk that is equally important, if much harder to eliminate. And that's longevity risk.

How old is the oldest living person in your family? Eighty? Ninety? One hundred?

There's a good chance you'll outlive that relative.

That's longevity risk.

Longevity risk is the risk of living too long, and it has a big impact on your retirement savings.

Longevity risk goes against the way you normally think. Most of us would agree a long life is a blessing. The longer you live, the more years you have to enjoy time with your children, grandchildren and, yes, great-grandchildren. My father-in-law turned ninety this year, and he treasures every day on earth as a gift.

But a long life also brings risks, and they're risks most of us don't think about.

Consider this. You're sixty-five and getting ready to retire. You're reviewing your retirement savings account to see how much money you'll have to spend in retirement. If you live to be eighty-five, those funds have to last twenty years. If you live to be ninety-five, that same pot of money has to last you thirty years. That's 50 percent more income needed from the same assets.

That's why longevity matters.

You're Probably Underestimating Your Lifespan

As an actuary, my specialty is in assessing longevity risk. When I would price insurance and annuity products for insurance companies, I would have to make assumptions about how long policyholders, on average, would live. Throughout my work, I found people often assume their longevity to be shorter than it is. Put another way, people almost always *under*estimate how long they'll live, and thus how much they need to save.

You don't have to take my word for it. There's a national organization called the Society of Actuaries, which is a leading research and education organization supporting actuaries like me. The Society of Actuaries conducted a survey where they asked Americans working today to estimate how long they would live. So go ahead and take a guess. How old do you think you'll get to be?

Here's the shocking outcome of the survey: 59 percent of people underestimated their longevity. Fifty-nine percent of people thought they would die sooner than is statistically likely.[20]

In other words, most people are underestimating how many years they'll spend retired, and because of that they're underestimating how much money they will need to support themselves in retirement.

---

[20] Society of Actuaries. June 2012. "2011 Risks and Process of Retirement Survey Report, Key Findings and Issues: Longevity." https://www.soa.org/files/research/projects/research-key-finding-longevity.pdf.

LIFE EXPECTANCY TABLE

	Men		Women	
Current Age	Expected Lifetime	Years Remaining	Expected Lifetime	Years Remaining
0	75.4	75.4	80.4	80.4
40	77.8	37.8	81.9	41.9
45	78.3	33.3	82.2	37.2
50	79.0	29.0	82.7	32.7
55	79.9	24.9	83.3	28.3
60	80.9	20.9	84.0	24.0
65	82.2	17.2	84.9	19.9
70	83.7	13.7	86.1	16.1
75	85.6	10.6	87.6	12.6
80	87.9	7.9	89.4	9.4
85	90.7	5.7	91.8	6.8
90	93.9	3.9	94.7	4.7
95	97.8	2.8	98.3	3.3
100	102.1	2.1	102.4	2.4

Society of Actuaries longevity table data provided by the Social Security Administration statistics.

The above table represents the average expected lifetime for each group specified. In the following pages, I'll explain why these numbers can be misleading.

Why Might You Live to be 100?

You've seen the headlines. The first person to live to 120 is likely alive today. Babies born today will be more likely than not to reach their ninetieth birthday.

There's a good chance you'll live longer than you think, too. Here are five reasons why:

No. 1 - You're reading those life expectancy numbers wrong (part I)

According to the Social Security Administration, life expectancy for men is seventy-four years and life expectancy for women is seventy-nine years. But that's life expectancy from birth. This includes everyone who dies at birth, in childhood, or as a young adult. When you look at life expectancy from age fifty, for example, you'll notice a bump. Life expectancy is now seventy-eight for men and eighty-two for women. Step it forward another fifteen years and consider life expectancy for someone who is sixty-five. A man is now expected to live to eighty-one, and a woman to eighty-four.

What does all this mean? Every year longer you live, your life expectancy goes down by a factor much smaller than one year. So if you make it to your fifties or sixties, you need to adjust your life expectancy assumptions accordingly.

No. 2 - You're reading those life expectancy numbers wrong (part II)

Let's further consider those life expectancy numbers. Remember, these are average numbers, and you're not average. Don't believe me? Consider this. Average life expectancy numbers are based on America's population as a whole. This includes people who smoke, people without access to adequate health care, people with cancer, people who don't wear their seat belts, and people who work dangerous jobs for a living. Chances are, you don't have most of those risk factors. Consider, too, that life expectancy and income correlate: higher income workers, on average, live longer than lower income workers.

The takeaway? If you live a healthy life, work a low-risk job, and take care of yourself, you're in a position to potentially beat the odds when it comes to longevity. So you need to plan for a longer life than the "average" American.

No. 3 - You're reading those life expectancy numbers wrong (part III)

This one's pretty basic, but it's often overlooked. Average life expectancy is just that: an average. That means you have a 50/50 chance of living longer than the number you see by your age.

No. 4 - Genes matter

When it comes to wearing your seat belt and not smoking, you can control some of your risk factors. But much of our longevity is determined by something we can't control: heredity.

How old is your oldest living relative? In her eighties? In his hundreds? Often I'll talk to people whose parents or grandparents all lived into their nineties. They have longevity in their genes.

If longevity runs in your family, it is absolutely something you need to plan for in your finances. That is the bottom line.

No. 5 - Modern medicine

Think about it. Your parents likely lived longer than their parents, who probably outlived their parents before them. Modern medicine is expanding lifespans. While it used to be rare to find many people in their eighties, today its commonplace. For people in their thirties, forties, fifties, or even sixties today, living into the nineties could be no big deal.

I see this in my own family every day. My wife's family has a history of heart disease. Her Grandpa Max died of a heart attack at the young age of fifty-six. Back in the 60s, there wasn't much doctors could do when someone suffered a massive heart attack.

But my wife's father, George, had a different story. He had the same genes for heart disease, but thanks to advances in medicine and a triple bypass surgery, his heart is still ticking at age ninety. Modern medicine made the difference.

I pray that my wife, kids, and grandkids don't get that same heredity for heart disease. But if they do, there's a good chance modern medicine can help them. Those bad genes won't be the death sentence they were to Grandpa Max in 1966.

In short, we can't base our longevity assumptions on the past, because the past didn't have access to our current medical environment. We have to base our longevity assumption on a forward projection that takes into account how long we're likely to live, not how long others like us have lived in the past.

Predict My Lifespan

There's no way to predict how long you'll live (if I had figured that out, I'd be a billionaire living on a beach somewhere). But there are some basic factors that can hint you may live a longer or shorter life.

Factors that may suggest a longer life:
- Grandparent or parent who lived to be 85+
- Low family history of cancer, heart attack and stroke
- Regular exercise
- Wearing your seat belt
- Eating a healthy diet
- Regular interaction with family and friends

Factors that may suggest a shorter life:
- Parents or grandparents who died before age 65 from a disease that is not preventable today
- Family history of cancer, heart attack or stroke
- Smoking
- Not wearing your seat belt
- Suffering from a chronic illness that negatively impacts your lifespan
- Sedentary lifestyle

Addressing Longevity Risk

There's an easy way to address longevity risk, though nobody likes it much: try to die before your mid-eighties.

Not too appealing, I know.

So, assuming you want to live a long and happy life, the best strategy is to plan like you'll live to age ninety-five.

Plan, Plan, Plan

Planning is the only thing that can address your longevity risk. You have to make sure the assumptions in your retirement plan reflect the realities of your life expectancy.

Because of this, I recommend that anyone under the age of sixty assume his or her retirement savings have to last until age ninety-five.

What does that mean to you? I'm going to use some very simplified math here to make a point. Let's say your plan is to accumulate $2 million by age sixty-five, when you want to retire. If you live until eighty-five, that money has to provide for 20 years. You could get a check for $100,000 a year without even earning any interest on your savings. Sounds good. Instead, let's say you live to be ninety-five. Now, that same pool of money has to last thirty years. And you're getting a check each year for $66,000. You've lost almost a third of your income.

There's no way to predict how long you will live. Even actuaries can only speak in generalities, not about you specifically (and you, specifically, are all that matters when it comes to saving). So plan for a long life. Make sure you are saving enough money to fund that long life.

Retired Thirty Years . . . and Counting

When Social Security was introduced in 1935, "retirement" was a very short phase of life. In 1940, only 60 percent of female workers even lived long enough to reach the retirement age of sixty-five. It was even lower for men. So Edna Mae might have retired at sixty-five, but only lived until seventy. She was only retired for five years before dying.

Now let's look at Edna Mae's great-granddaughter, Rachel, in 1990. Rachel has nearly an 84 percent chance of making it to retirement age of sixty-five.[21] Much better. And she's likely to live an average of twenty years in retirement, to age eighty-five. That's a retirement that's four times longer than her grandmother.

So Rachel's retirement savings better last about four times longer, too.

And when *you* go to retire in 2020, or 2050, the numbers are going to be even higher. There's a good chance you'll live thirty or more years in retirement. That means your savings has to last dramatically longer.

Of course, the only way to completely eliminate longevity risk is to die young, and I'm certainly not advocating for that. Short of dying young, your best strategy is to make sure you save enough money to support yourself for at least thirty years in retirement.

How much money will that take?

Give Me a Dollar Amount.

Alright, I promised to help you figure out how much you need to accumulate by retirement. I'm going to keep to that promise.

Below is a simple way to estimate how much you'll need, in real dollar amounts, at age sixty-five to fund your retirement. I've

---

[21] Social Security Administration. "Social Security History: Life Expectancy for Social Security." http://www.ssa.gov/history/lifeexpect.html.

broken it down into two steps and included a worksheet area in each section where you can create an estimate for your own situation.

Step 1: Estimate how much income (adjusted for inflation) you'll need each year in retirement.

Take an educated guess about what kind of income you will need each year in retirement. As we discussed earlier in the book, many experts recommend a minimum of 70 percent of your pre-retirement income. However, keep in mind many active retirees spend just as much in retirement as when they worked.

Figure out the amount of annual income you want in today's dollars, and then add about 2 percent per year (from now until your retirement date) to account for inflation. To make it easy, I've added an inflation "multiple" for a range of ages. Pick the one closest to your age, and just multiply your annual income number by that amount.

AGE	MULTIPLE
25	2.21
30	2.0
35	1.81
40	1.64
45	1.49

If you save for retirement in a qualified plan, like a 401(k) or IRA, you'll need to figure in taxes, too. It's impossible to know what your tax rate will be when you retire, but it's a safe bet to add 25 to 30 percent to cover state, local, and federal taxes.

Following is an example for my thirty-nine-year-old daughter Rebecca, and a space to work out your personal numbers as well.

REBECCA:

Annual Income Needed (in today's dollars)	$80,000
(x) Inflation Multiple of 1.81	$144,800
(+) 30% for taxation (Only if in a taxable account like a 401(k) or IRA. This calculation is not needed for funds in IUL or Roths.)	$188,240
TOTAL ANNUAL INCOME NEEDED IN RETIREMENT	**$188,240**

YOU:

Annual Income Needed (in today's dollars)	
(x) Inflation Multiple	
(+) 30% for taxation (Only if in a taxable account like a 401(k) or IRA. This calculation is not needed for funds in IUL or Roths.)	
TOTAL ANNUAL INCOME NEEDED IN RETIREMENT	

Step 2: Estimate the amount of funds required to meet your annual income need.

Here's where retirement income planning can get a little wonky, so I'll make it as easy to understand as possible.

Essentially, we want to answer this question: How big does my account have to be to deliver $188,240 (or whatever your annual income number from above turns out to be) every year for the rest of my life?

There could be a lot of variables that go into this calculation. After all, even when you start withdrawing funds from your account, the remaining funds still can grow, most likely at a very conservative rate.

So I've found the easiest thing to do is ask: If I wanted to buy an annuity that would deliver $188,240 (or your number) of annual income for the rest of my life, how much money would I need to buy it?

If you're not familiar with annuities, I'll take a quick detour to explain. Annuities are essentially insurance contracts that deliver a set amount of annual payment for the rest of your life, no matter how long you live. If that sounds like a pension, you're right. Annuities are essentially a way for savers without a pension to purchase guaranteed annual income from their 401(k) or IRA.

For most people over sixty-five, chances are at least some of their retirement funds are in an annuity. They're a very common way to withdraw income from retirement savings.

Now, I'm not encouraging you to go out and buy an annuity. But it's a simple way to calculate how much money you would need to lock in a set income for your entire retirement.

Back to our example. If you want to make sure you have $188,240 (or, of course, your number) every year for the rest of your life, you could purchase an immediate annuity that would deliver that amount of income every year until you die.

So how much would you need in your account to purchase that annuity?

A general rule of thumb is you need fifteen times the amount of income you want to receive to purchase that annuity. There are plenty of websites you can visit for a more exact factor, but remember we're just estimating here, so I feel confident you can use a factor of fifteen.

For my daughter Rebecca's example before, that would mean:

Annual Income Needed in Retirement	$188,240
(x) Annuity Factor	(x) 15
Total Account Value Needed at Age 65	**$2.82 Million**

Try your own:

Annual Income Needed in Retirement	$
(x) Annuity Factor	(x) 15
Total Account Value Needed at Age 65	$

Yes, that's a lot of money. But now you know the strategy that can help you get there.

The Power of Now

The number above stresses how important it is to start saving the right way now. Not a year from now or when you get around to it, but right now. Today. This week. This month.

Decisions, especially financial decisions, are easy to put off. But look at your number. You may have a long way to go to accumulate that much money, and you don't want to depend on contributions to reach it. You want to depend on compound interest and growth.

Deciding to save right now can maximize your compound interest. As the last hundred pages have shown, IUL can help you maximize the rest.

Now you know the New Rules of Retirement Saving. Go put them to work!

ABOUT THE AUTHOR

Martin H. Ruby is a native of Louisville, Kentucky, where he lives and works. An actuary by profession, Martin serves as founder and CEO of Stonewood Financial. The company delivers actuarial expertise to clients building and managing wealth. In addition to serving his clients, Martin serves as a mentor for financial advisors adding tax-efficient planning to their practices, and he speaks nationally about the importance of tax-free income for today's retirees.

Before starting his own firm, Martin was CEO of a multi-billion-dollar insurance and annuity company, Integrity Life, where he led the growth of a successful retail annuity business, cutting-edge technology platforms, and innovative product development. He also served as head of the Life and Annuity Industry Group for Channel Point Technology and in several senior executive positions for Capital Holding Corporation (now part of AEGON).

Martin is a Fellow of the Society of Actuaries (FSA). He holds a Master of Business Administration degree from Bellarmine University and a Bachelor of Science degree in mathematics from Purdue University.

A dedicated community member, Martin has chaired and served on numerous boards for nonprofit and for-profit organizations, including Louisville Metro United Way, Jewish Hospital and the Louisville Jewish Community Center. He is an active Angel Investor for start-up companies and enjoys mentoring emerging entrepreneurs.

Martin is married to his wife, Michele, who he met in first grade. They grew up together through junior high school and were in the same graduating class at Seneca High School in 1968. They married in 1971 and have two adult daughters, Becky and Sara. Both daughters are married to men both named Michael. Martin and Michele have been blessed with four grandchildren: Robert, Molly, Andrew, and George.

Martin gained an interest in the savings industry through his parents, Bob and Tess Ruby. Both were children of the Great Depression who instilled a strong work ethic and saving habit in their children. Bob and Tess put an emphasis on preparing for the future and valuing time spent with family. Martin works to accomplish these two goals every day in his life, as well.

ACKNOWLEDGMENTS

It's an honor and a privilege to share my passion with you, the reader. I hope this book will set you on a better path to financial security. But I didn't do it alone. I want to thank several people who made this book possible. First, my daughter, Becky, who not only served as an inspiration for me to help the next generation save, but who helped me craft this book. She took my actuarial insights and turned them into stories that would move readers like you. I'd like to thank my wife, Michele, a poet and author who helped make sure this book spoke to people with a wide range of financial knowledge. And finally, I'd like to thank all of my friends, colleagues, and clients who were worried their friends and children weren't saving well for the future; their concerns became this book.

Made in the USA
Middletown, DE
13 April 2019